The NEWAY™ COOKBOOK

Premier Edition

Barbara Isaac Croce
and the entire NEWAY™ family

*This book is dedicated to
my best friend
and the love of my life,
my husband Rich,
who continually believes in me
and encourages me
to do the impossible
for the glory of God.
Thank you.*

May we continue to have fun cooking the NEWAY™ together!

*"Whether, then, you eat or drink or whatever you do,
do all to the glory of God." 1 Cor. 10:31*

CONTENTS

Going Meatless (15)

I still love meat, but I have discovered lately that I don't need it every day. There are plenty of meatless recipes that fulfill my needs for protein and make my taste buds happy.

Salads, Both Light and Serious, and Dressings Too (32)

Eating the NEWAY™ way catapulted me into the world of salads. I can hardly have enough of these, but I like variety every day. So here I have a plethora of choices for you. You can even use your imagination, mix them together, add interesting flavors and textures, or create your own!

Side Dishes (22)

One of the greatest challenges when someone embarks on the NEWAY™ lifestyle is to eat enough vegetable portions in a day. I have given you plenty of choices here so you won't possibly get bored—and you will find these quite enjoyable.

Breakfast Anytime: Eggs, Breads, Muffins and All That Good Stuff (16)

Breakfast has surely become my favorite meal. But I am a big fan of diversity, so here are lots of fun and tasty choices.

Sweet Tooth for All (32)

I love to sit down to a lovely little cookie, or piece of pie once in a while, and savor every bite. I have tweaked lots of traditional recipes for you, so you can have your cake and eat it too—without any guilt.

Drinks (6)

Most of the time I want to eat my calories, not drink them, but there are exceptions to every rule. Here are some worthy ones.

Index

Introduction

NEWAY™: Nutrition, Exercise, Wisdom, Attitude and You!

Always plump, never quite good enough… that was the story of the lady in the mirror in my life.

When I eventually accepted that I was made to live and eat God's way, NEWAY™ just kind of birthed itself—and I got rid of the fat that seemed to define me more than it ought to. My body came into simple balance for the first time in my life, and I have felt wonderful ever since.

I have taken many people with me in my NEWAY™ journey, and we have enjoyed discovering exciting new foods along the way. We have had "recipe challenges" in order to create suitable ones; we have taken many traditional recipes and tweaked them. Just for fun, we made up lots of new ones as well.

In order to be NEWAY™ worthy, a recipe must adhere to these simple criteria:
~It uses no artificial ingredients—"nonfoods" we call them
~It has just about no refined ingredients
~It gives our taste buds something to talk about
~It chooses low-glycemic-index ingredients as often as possible

It is with great joy that I present to you the fruit of the NEWAY™ test kitchens of America: the premier edition of the NEWAY™ Cookbook. I expect these 215 recipes will give *your* taste buds something to smile about.

To your health,

Barbara Isaac Croce and the whole NEWAY™ family.

Appetizers,
Salty Snacks,
and Salsas

"Cooking is like love.
It should be entered into with abandon or not at all."
Harriet van Horne

DIPS

Baba Ghanouj

INGREDIENTS:
2 cups roasted eggplant (put eggplant halves in preheated 425 oven on cookie sheet for 30 minutes; let cool)
2 tablespoons fresh parsley, chopped
1 tablespoon white wine vinegar
1 tablespoon tahini paste
2 cloves garlic, minced
2 teaspoon olive oil
1 teaspoon cumin
Dash of red pepper flakes
1 teaspoon kosher salt

DIRECTIONS:
Put all ingredients in food processor. Process until it is all mixed together and smooth. Let stand at room temperature about 1 hour to blend flavors.

NUTRITIONAL INFORMATION:
Servings: 8 (1/4 cup each)
Calories: 53
Total Fat: 4 g (68 %)
Total Carbohydrates: 4 g (27 %)
Dietary Fiber: 1.5 g
Protein: 1 g (5 %)

NOTES: *Great with zucchini sticks, pita chips and carrot sticks.*

INGREDIENTS:
1 large eggplant
½ cup walnut pieces
2 teaspoons fresh gingerroot, peeled, grated, and finely chopped
2 cloves garlic, mashed
1 tablespoon extra-virgin olive oil
¼ teaspoon ground allspice
Salt and hot pepper sauce to taste

DIRECTIONS:
Preheat oven to 450 degrees F. Pierce the eggplant with a fork in several places and bake until very soft, about 45 minutes. While the eggplant is baking, grind the walnuts in a food processor until very fine. Remove the eggplant from oven, slash to let steam escape, drain off any liquid, and scrape the pulp into a food processor with the gingerroot, garlic, and olive oil. Process until smooth. Add the ground walnuts and allspice, season to taste with the salt and hot pepper sauce and process again until smooth. Spoon into a small loaf dish and chill several hours or until firm.

NUTRITIONAL INFORMATION:
Servings: 16
Calories: 41
Total Fat: 3.5 g (70 %)
Total Carbohydrates: 2.5 g (23 %)
Dietary Fiber: 1 g
Protein: 1 g (7 %)

NOTES:

INGREDIENTS:
½ cup (4 ounces) fat-free ricotta cheese
¼ cup fat-free sour cream
2 tablespoons orange juice
1 package (10 ounces) frozen chopped spinach, thawed and squeezed dry
¼ cup chopped green onions
¼ cup chopped fresh basil
2 tablespoons chopped fresh oregano
2 cloves garlic, minced
¼ teaspoon ground nutmeg
Dash of hot-pepper sauce
Sea salt and freshly ground black pepper

DIRECTIONS:
In food processor, combine the ricotta cheese, sour cream and orange juice. Add spinach, green onions, basil, oregano, garlic, nutmeg and hot-pepper sauce. Process until smooth, stopping occasionally to scrape down the sides of the container. Add salt and pepper to taste. Pour into a medium bowl, cover and refrigerate at least 30 minutes or overnight.

NUTRITIONAL INFORMATION:
Servings: 32 (1 tablespoon)
Calories: 7
Total Fat: 0 g (2 %)
Total Carbohydrates: 1 g (59 %)
Dietary Fiber: 0.5 g
Protein: 0.5 g (35 %)

NOTES:

Guacamole

INGREDIENTS:
2 ripe avocados
1 plum tomato, diced
½ teaspoon grated lime zest
1 ½ teaspoon freshly squeezed lime juice
1 small garlic clove, minced
½ serrano chili pepper, seeded and minced (optional)
Sea salt

DIRECTIONS:
Cut each avocado in half lengthwise. Twist halves to separate. Remove and discard pits.
Scoop avocado meat into bowl and mash coarsely wit a fork. Add tomato, lime zest, juice,
garlic and chili pepper. Mix well and season with salt.

NUTRITIONAL INFORMATION:
Servings: 20 (1 tablespoon)
Calories: 29
Total Fat: 2.5 g (76 %)
Total Carbohydrates: 1.5 g (20 %)
Dietary Fiber: 1 g
Protein: 0 g (4 %)

NOTES: Great with baked tortillas.

INGREDIENTS:
1-15 ounce can garbanzo beans, liquid reserved
2 ounces fresh jalapeno pepper, sliced
½ teaspoon ground cumin
2 tablespoons lemon juice
3 cloves garlic, minced
Dash of salt and black pepper

DIRECTIONS:
In a blender or food processor, combine all ingredients and 1 to 3 tablespoons of reserved liquid. Blend until smooth.

NUTRITIONAL INFORMATION:
Servings: 16
Calories: 34
Total Fat: 0.5 g (6 %)
Total Carbohydrates: 6.5 g (91 %)
Dietary Fiber: 4 g
Protein: 1.5 g (4 %)

NOTES:

SALTY SNACKS

Baked Tortilla Chips

INGREDIENTS:
1-12 ounce package of corn tortillas
1 tablespoon olive oil
3 tablespoons lime juice
1 ½ teaspoons ground cumin
1 ½ teaspoons chili powder
Nonstick cooking spray
1 teaspoon salt

DIRECTIONS:
Preheat oven to 375 degrees F.
Cut each tortilla into 8 chip-sized wedges and arrange the wedges in a single layer on a cookie sheet sprayed with nonstick cooking spray.
In a mister, combine oil and lime juice. Mix well and spray each tortilla wedge until slightly moist. Combine cumin, chili powder and salt and sprinkle on chips. Bake for about 7 minutes. Rotate pan and bake for another 8 minutes or until chips are crisp, but not too brown. Serve with salsa, garnishes or guacamole.

NUTRITIONAL INFORMATION:
Servings: 6 (18 wedges)
Calories: 150
Total Fat: 4 g (23 %)
Total Carbohydrates: 27 g (64 %)
Dietary Fiber: 1g
Protein: 3.5 g (9 %)

NOTES:

INGREDIENTS:
1 cup cooked, chopped spinach
¾ cup fat-free cottage cheese
1 teaspoon ground nutmeg
2 egg whites
2 tablespoons grated Parmesan cheese
Salt and black pepper
Nonstick cooking spray

DIRECTIONS:
Preheat oven to 425 degrees F. Spray 6 ramekin dishes with nonstick cooking spray. Mix together spinach and cottage cheese in a small bowl, then add nutmeg and salt and pepper to taste. Whisk the egg whites in a separate bowl until stiff enough to hold soft peaks. Fold them evenly into the spinach mixture using a spatula or large metal spoon, then spoon mixture into the ramekins. Smooth the tops and sprinkle with Parmesan. Place on a baking sheet.
Bake for 15-20 minutes, or until puffed and golden brown. Serve immediately.

NUTRITIONAL INFORMATION:
Servings: 6
Calories: 40
Total Fat: 0.5 g (13 %)
Total Carbohydrates: 2.5 g (24 %)
Dietary Fiber: 1 g
Protein: 6 g (58 %)

NOTES:

INGREDIENTS:
5 medium zucchini
4 ounces Blue Cheese, crumbled
3 tablespoons grated Parmesan cheese
1 ½ teaspoons dried basil
⅛ teaspoon pepper
18 cherry tomatoes, halved

DIRECTIONS:
Cut zucchini into 36 slices. Using small spoon, scoop out the insides and discard, leaving bottom intact. Place zucchini on an ungreased baking sheet; spoon ½ teaspoon crumbled blue cheese into each. Combine parmesan, basil and pepper; sprinkle half over blue cheese. Top each with half a cherry tomato. Sprinkle with remaining parmesan mixture. Bake at 400 degrees for 5-7 minutes or until cheese is melted. Serve warm.

NUTRITIONAL INFORMATION:
Servings: 36
Calories: 19
Total Fat: 1 g (50 %)
Total Carbohydrates: 1.5 g (27 %)
Dietary Fiber: 0.5 g
Protein: 1 g (46 %)

NOTES:

Lime Tortilla Chips

INGREDIENTS:
Nonstick cooking spray
1 teaspoon grated lime peel
2 tablespoons fresh-squeezed lime juice
2 teaspoons olive oil
1 teaspoon honey
4 whole wheat tortillas (8" diameter)
Chili powder, to taste

DIRECTIONS:
Heat oven to 350 degrees F and spray a large cookie sheet with nonstick cooking spray.
In a medium sized bowl, combine lime peel, lime juice, chili pepper, oil, and honey, and stir
thoroughly. Using a pizza cutter, cut tortillas into 12 wedges. Place wedges on a single layer
on cookie sheet. Brush the tortillas wedges with the lime mixture, using a pastry brush.
Sprinkle with chili powder to desired amount. Bake for 8-10 minutes or until golden brown.

NUTRITIONAL INFORMATION:
Servings: 6
Calories: 78
Total Fat: 3 g (19 %)
Total Carbohydrates: 16 g (64 %)
Dietary Fiber: 3 g
Protein: 2.5 g (14 %)

NOTES:

INGREDIENTS:
8 ounces Gruyere cheese, shredded
8 ounces reduced-fat Swiss cheese, shredded
1 cup dry white wine
1 can (15 ounces) white beans, rinsed and drained
2 large cloves of garlic
1 tablespoon Dijon mustard
1 tablespoon lemon juice

DIRECTIONS:
In a food processor, combine beans, mustard, garlic, lemon juice and half the wine. Process until smooth.
Heat this mixture in saucepan until simmering. Add remaining wine, then add ¼ of the cheese at a time, stirring well to ensure it melts before adding more cheese. Once cheese has melted, transfer to your fondue pot. (NOTE: Ceramic fondue pots are better for cheese fondue)

NUTRITIONAL INFORMATION:
Servings: 12 (1/2 cup cheese mixture)
Calories: 162
Total Fat: 7 g (39 %)
Total Carbohydrates: 8 g (20 %)
Dietary Fiber: 1.5 g
Protein: 13 g (33 %)

NOTES: Serve with blanched broccoli, cauliflower, asparagus, or carrots, chunks of whole-grain bread and breadsticks, grilled chicken or turkey chunks, raw mushrooms, pepper strips or cocktail onions.

Roasted Portabella with Blue Cheese

INGREDIENTS:
2 large Portabella mushrooms, stems removed
1 tablespoon soy sauce, or to taste
Freshly ground black pepper
1 ounce crumbled Blue Cheese

DIRECTIONS:
Preheat oven or toaster oven to 425 degrees F.
Place mushroom caps, gill side up, on baking sheet. Drizzle with soy sauce and add a few grinds of black pepper to each cap.
Bake for 25 minutes. Remove from oven, and sprinkle with Blue Cheese. Return to oven and bake an additional 10 minutes, or until cheese is fully melted.

NUTRITIONAL INFORMATION:
Servings: 2
Calories: 79
Total Fat: 4.5 g (47 %)
Total Carbohydrates: 6 g (27 %)
Dietary Fiber: 1.5 g
Protein: 6 g (26 %)

NOTES:

Spiced Pecans

INGREDIENTS:
2 tablespoons maple syrup
1 tablespoon Worcestershire sauce
2 teaspoons chili powder
1 teaspoon cumin
½ teaspoon salt
½ teaspoon black pepper
2 cups pecan halves

DIRECTIONS:
Preheat oven to 375 degrees F. Combine maple syrup, Worcestershire sauce, chili powder, cumin, salt and pepper in large bowl, stirring well. Add nuts and toss well to coat. Arrange nuts in a single layer on a jelly-roll pan lines with parchment paper. Bake for 10 minutes or until lightly browned. Cool completely on pan.

NUTRITIONAL INFORMATION:
Servings: 16 (2 tablespoons)
Calories: 100
Total Fat: 10 g (81 %)
Total Carbohydrates: 4 g (14 %)
Dietary Fiber: 1 g
Protein: 1.5 g (4 %)

NOTES:

INGREDIENTS:
10 ounces frozen chopped spinach
⅛ teaspoon salt
8 large mushrooms
1 tablespoon olive oil

DIRECTIONS:
In medium saucepan, bring ½ cup water to a boil. Add spinach and salt, cover and cook according to package directions. Wash mushrooms and remove stems. Trim of ends of stems and chop them.
Heat olive oil in large skillet. Add chopped mushroom stems; saute until golden, about 3 minutes. Remove from pan. Add mushroom caps to the skillet and saute 4-5 minutes. Remove mushroom caps to a heatproof platter.
Drain spinach. Stir in sauteed chopped mushroom stems. Spoon spinach mixture into caps and serve immediately or place in oven on low heat to keep warm.

NUTRITIONAL INFORMATION:
Servings: 8
Calories: 28
Total Fat: 2 g (57 %)
Total Carbohydrates: 2.5 g (30 %)
Dietary Fiber: 1 g
Protein: 1.5 g (14 %)

NOTES:

SALSAS

Black Bean Salsa

INGREDIENTS:
3 (15 ounce) cans black beans, drained and rinsed
1 (11 ounce) can of corn, strained
2 (10 ounce) cans of diced tomatoes with green chili peppers, partially drained
1 (28 ounces) can of diced tomatoes
1 bunch of green onions, chopped

DIRECTIONS:
In large bowl, mix all ingredients together. Refrigerate at least 8 hours to blend flavors.

NUTRITIONAL INFORMATION:
Servings: 50 (1/4 cup)
Calories: 31
Fat: 0 g (7 %)
Total Carbohydrates: 6 g (74 %)
Dietary Fiber: 2 g
Protein: 2 g (18 %)

NOTES:

Corn Relish

INGREDIENTS:
3 ½ cups corn kernels
1 cup finely diced red onion
1 cup finely chopped parsley
3 tablespoons lime juice
1 tablespoon olive oil
½ teaspoon salt
½ teaspoon chili powder

DIRECTIONS:
Combine corn, onion, parsley, lime juice, oil and salt in a medium bowl. Serve at room temperature or cold.

NUTRITIONAL INFORMATION:
Servings: 12 (1/3 cup each)
Calories: 66
Total Fat: 3 g (37 %)
Total Carbohydrates: 10 g (57 %)
Dietary Fiber: 0.5 g
Protein: 1.5 g (6 %)

NOTES:

DIRECTIONS:
1 grapefruit, sectioned
1 avocado, diced
Cilantro to taste
1 small onion, diced
1 clove garlic, minced
Sea salt to taste

DIRECTIONS:
Mix.

NUTRITIONAL INFORMATION:
Servings: 4
Calories: 99
Total Fat: 7 g (64 %)
Total Carbohydrates: 10 g (28 %)
Dietary Fiber: 3 g
Protein: 2 g (8 %)

NOTES: Variation: substitute tomatoes for grapefruit

Mango-Papaya Salsa
Submitted by Holley Belch

INGREDIENTS:
1 mango, peeled, seeded and diced
1 medium papaya, peeled, seeded and diced
1 medium red pepper, seeded and diced
1 avocado, peeled, pitted and diced
½ cup red onion, peeled and finely diced
2 tablespoons chopped cilantro
2 tablespoons balsamic vinegar
Salt and pepper to taste

DIRECTIONS:
In medium bowl, gently toss mango, papaya, red bell pepper, avocado, sweet onion, cilantro and balsamic vinegar. Add salt and pepper to taste. Cover and chill until ready to serve.

NUTRITIONAL INFORMATION:
Servings: 8
Calories: 75
Total Fat: 3.5 g (39 %)
Total Carbohydrates: 12 g (57 %)
Dietary Fiber: 2.75 g
Protein: 1 g (4 %)

NOTES: Great with fish!

Nadene's Salsa Fresca
Submitted by Nadene L'Amoreaux

INGREDIENTS:
2 ½ cups diced tomatoes
1 cob fresh corn kernels, uncooked
2 teaspoons cider vinegar
½ bunch fresh parsley, roughly chopped
½ large onion, diced
1 medium jalapeno pepper, finely diced
3 large garlic cloves, minced

DIRECTIONS:
Toss all ingredients together, salt to taste and serve.

NUTRITIONAL INFORMATION:
Serving: ¼ cup
Calories: 11
Total Fat: 0 g (9 %)
Total Carbohydrates: 2.5 g (82 %)
Dietary Fiber: 0 g
Protein: 0.5 g (10 %)

NOTES:

Peach Salsa
Submitted by Claudine Bothell

INGREDIENTS:
4 large peaches, peeled and diced
¼ cup raisins
¼ cup red onion, diced
1 tablespoon lemon juice

DIRECTIONS:
Combine ingredients and refrigerate several hours.

NUTRITIONAL INFORMATION:
Serving: ¼ cup
Calories: 36
Total Fat: 0 g (2 %)
Total Carbohydrates: 9.5 g (93 %)
Dietary Fiber: 1 g
Protein: 0.5 g (4 %)

NOTES: Great with fish, chicken or pita bread.

INGREDIENTS:
4 cups diced seedless watermelon
1 cup diced green pepper
1 cup diced sweet red pepper
1 cup diced red onion
2 cup sliced carrots
2 jalapeno peppers, seeded and cut into rings
2 tablespoons rice wine vinegar
1 tablespoon olive oil
1 cup chopped fresh cilantro
2 tablespoons chopped fresh mint
2 tablespoons chopped fresh basil
¼ cup unsalted chopped peanuts

DIRECTIONS:
In large bowl, combine all ingredients but peanuts. Cover and refrigerate. Just before serving, sprinkle with peanuts.

NUTRITIONAL INFORMATION:
Servings: 34 (1/4 cup servings)
Calories: 22
Total Fat: 1 g (41 %)
Total Carbohydrates: 3 g (36 %)
Dietary Fiber: 1 g
Protein: 1 g (18 %)

NOTES:

Soups, both Hot and Cold

"As the days grow short, some faces grow long.
But not mine.
Every autumn, when the wind turns cold and darkness comes
early,
I am suddenly happy.
It's time to start making soup again."
Leslie Newman

HOT SOUPS

Asparagus Soup

INGREDIENTS:
1 tablespoon olive oil
½ cup finely chopped carrots
½ cup finely chopped celery
½ cup finely chopped onions
Salt to taste
Freshly ground black pepper
1 quart vegetable broth
5 cups chopped asparagus stalks
Fresh dill to taste (optional)

DIRECTIONS:
Heat the olive oil in a saucepan over low heat. Add the carrots, celery and onion, season lightly with salt and pepper, and cook for 10 minutes. Add the stock and bring to a boil quickly over high heat. Lower the heat and simmer until the vegetables are tender, about 15 minutes. Add the asparagus and simmer until just tender, about 5 to 7 minutes. Process in blender until smooth. Add the dill if desired. Adjust the salt and pepper to taste.
Optional: Add a dollop of low-fat sour cream to each portion.

NUTRITIONAL INFORMATION:
Servings: 6 (1 cup)
Calories: 59
Total Fat: 3 g (34 %)
Total Carbohydrates: 7 g (42 %)
Dietary Fiber: 3 g
Protein: 7 g (25 %)

NOTES:

INGREDIENTS:
1 tablespoon olive oil
1 large red onion, sliced
1 large white onion, sliced
1 leek (white and light green part only), sliced
Salt and freshly ground pepper to taste
2 cans (14.5 ounces) of fat-free chicken broth
4 cups water
Salt and freshly ground pepper (optional)
¼ cup grated low-fat Swiss cheese (optional)
1 bunch chives, finely chopped (optional)

DIRECTIONS:
Heat oil in large saucepan over medium-high heat. Add onions and cook 5 minutes, stirring occasionally. Stir in leek; turn temperature to low and continue cooking until all onions are caramelized and golden brown, about 25 minutes. Add stock, water and simmer uncovered 15 minutes. Season to taste. Ladle into shallow bowls; garnish with cheese and chives, if desired.

NUTRITIONAL INFORMATION:
Servings: 6
Calories: 48 (without cheese)
Fat: 2.5 g (38 %)
Total Carbohydrates: 6.5 g (46 %)
Dietary Fiber: 1 g
Protein: 0.5 g (5 %)

NOTES:

Cauliflower Bisque

INGREDIENTS:
1 tablespoon olive oil
1 cup diced onion
6 cups fat-free chicken broth
8 cups cauliflower flowerets (about 1 head)
1 teaspoon paprika
3 tablespoons half-and-half
Sea salt and nutmeg, dash of cayenne

DIRECTION:
In large saucepan, heat olive oil over medium heat. Add onion and cook, stirring, until softened, about 3 minutes. Pour in broth and bring to a boil. Reduce and simmer for about 5 minutes. Add cauliflower and paprika, continue to cook for 15 minutes more. Add half-and-half to the soup. Puree in pot or in food processor. Season to taste with nutmeg, sea salt and cayenne pepper.

NUTRITIONAL INFORMATION:
Servings: 9 (1 cup each)
Calories: 54
Total Fat: 3.5 g (38 %)
Total Carbohydrates: 10 g (45 %)
Dietary Fiber: 4 g
Protein: 4 g (16 %)

NOTES:

INGREDIENTS:
2 cup fat free chicken stock
2 cups water
6 cups chopped broccoli (about 1 large bunch)
2 clove garlic, minced
1 tablespoon grated ginger root
1 cup evaporated skimmed milk
2 tablespoons soy sauce
¼ cup finely chopped red onion

DIRECTIONS:
In a large saucepan, bring broth to a boil. Add the chopped broccoli, garlic and ginger.
Reduce the heat to low and cover. Steam for about 5 minutes or until the broccoli is tender.
Remove from the heat.   After the broccoli has cooled slightly, puree it in a food processor or
blender. Return it to the sauce pan. Add milk and soy sauce. Warm over low heat.   Serve
sprinkled with chopped red onion.

NUTRITIONAL INFORMATION:
Servings: 4
Per Serving: 75
Fat: 0.5 g (7 %)
Total Carbohydrates: 15 g (63 %)
Dietary Fiber: 4.5 g
Protein: 7 g (31 %)

NOTES:

INGREDIENTS:
2 large sweet potatoes (4 cups cooked cubes)
4 cups fat-free chicken broth
1 tablespoon butter
1 tablespoon whole wheat flour
½ teaspoon ground ginger
12 oz. fat-free evaporated milk
2 tablespoons chopped pecans

DIRECTIONS:
Preheat oven to 400ºF. Pierce potatoes in several places with a fork. Bake for 45 minutes, remove from oven and allow to cool--or simply microwave potatoes until cooked. When cool, remove and discard skin; chop potatoes.
Combine sweet potatoes and 3/4 cup of broth in a blender or food processor; blend or process until smooth, about 1 minute. Set potato mixture aside. Melt butter in a saucepan; stir in flour and ginger, and then add milk. Cook, stirring, until slightly thickened and bubbly, about 5 minutes. Cook 1 minute more and then stir in sweet potato mixture and remaining 1 ¼ cups of broth. Cook, stirring, until heated through, about 5 minutes more.
Pour into serving bowls and sprinkle each with ¾ teaspoon of pecans.

NUTRITIONAL INFORMATION:
Servings: 8 (1 cup)
Calories: 118
Total Fat: 4.5 g (34 %)
Total Carbohydrates: 15 g (52 %)
Dietary Fiber: 2 g
Protein: 4 g (17 %)

NOTES:

INGREDIENTS:
2 slices turkey bacon
½ cup finely chopped onion
¼ cup finely chopped celery
2 garlic cloves, crushed
2 cups fat free chicken broth
3 tablespoons whole wheat flour
½ cup potatoes, finely diced
1 10-ounce can whole baby clams
2 cups 2 % milk
Nonstick cooking spray

DIRECTIONS:
Place bacon in skillet and cook until crisp. Set aside. Spray skillet with nonstick cooking spray. Add onion and celery. Cook until tender, but do not brown. Add garlic, mix and set aside. Place chicken broth in saucepan, but save 3-4 tablespoons and mix them with the flour. Let broth come to a boil and add broth with flour mixture. Continue to boil and stir until liquid is smooth and begins to thicken. Add potato and simmer until tender. Stir in onion, celery and garlic. Add clams and milk. Simmer for 5-10 minutes. Garnish with crumbled bacon.

NUTRITIONAL INFORMATION:
Servings: 6
Calories: 123
Total Fat: 3 g (23 %)
Total Carbohydrates: 12.5 g (40 %)
Dietary Fiber: 1 g
Protein: 11 g (37 %)

NOTES:

INGREDIENTS:
4 large red bell peppers, seeded and chopped
1 large onion, chopped
1 teaspoon olive oil
2 garlic cloves, minced
1 small red chili, sliced
3 tablespoons tomato paste
4 cups fat-free chicken broth
Finely grated rind and juice of 1 lime
Salt and black pepper
Shreds of lime rind, to garnish

DIRECTIONS:
Cook onion and bell peppers gently in the oil in a covered saucepan for 5 minutes, shaking the pan occasionally, until softened. Stir in garlic, then add chili with tomato paste. Stir in half the broth and bring to a boil. Cover pan and simmer for 10 minutes. Cool slightly, then puree in food processor. Return to pan and add remaining broth, lime rind and juice and seasoning. Bring soup back to a boil and serve at once with a few strips of lime rind scattered in each bowl.

NUTRITIONAL INFORMATION:
Servings: 4
Calories: 90
Fat: 2 g (16 %)
Carbohydrates: 19 g (71 %)
Dietary Fiber: 5 g
Protein: 4 g (16 %)

NOTES:

INGREDIENTS:
1 large onion, cut into large chunks
1 large carrot, peeled and cut into 1 ½-inch pieces
3 cups sliced parsnips
4 cups winter squash, such as butternut, peeled and cubed
Nonstick cooking spray
4 cups fat-free chicken broth
½ cup fat-free evaporated milk
½ teaspoon sea salt, or to taste
½ teaspoon freshly ground black pepper, or to taste

DIRECTION:
Preheat oven to 400ºF. In a large roasting pan, combine onion, carrots, parsnips and squash; coat with nonstick cooking spray. Roast for 15 minutes. Place vegetables in a large pot. Add broth and milk; season to taste with salt and pepper. Cook over medium-high heat for 10 minutes to allow flavors to combine. Transfer mixture to a blender or food processor and blend until smooth.

NUTRITIONAL INFORMATION:
Servings: 8 (1 ½ cups)
Calories: 80
Total Fat: 0.5 g (5 %)
Total Carbohydrates: 17.5 g (81 %)
Dietary Fiber: 4 g
Protein: 3 g (13 %)

NOTES:

INGREDIENTS:
1 16-ounce package of frozen leaf spinach
1 large sweet potato (8 ounces), peeled and diced
1 large carrot (12 ounces), shredded
1 cup onion, coarsely chopped
2 garlic cloves, minced
1 can (14.5 ounces) fat free chicken broth
6 cups water
½ teaspoon freshly ground black pepper
½ teaspoon salt
¼ teaspoon nutmeg
8 tablespoons grated Parmesan cheese
Red bell pepper, slivered

DIRECTIONS:
In large sauce pan, combine spinach, potato, carrot, scallions, garlic, diluted broth, pepper, nutmeg and salt. Cover and bring to a boil over high heat, then reduce the heat to medium-low and simmer until the potato and carrot are tender, about 15 minutes.
Ladle soup into bowls and sprinkle with 1 tablespoon Parmesan per bowl. Garnish with the bell pepper.

NUTRITIONAL INFORMATION:
Servings: 8 (1 ¼ cups)
Per Serving: 67 Calories
Total Fat: 2.5 g (25 %)
Total Carbohydrates: 7 g (19 %)
Dietary Fiber: 4 g
Protein: 5 g (35 %)

NOTES:

INGREDIENTS:
1 cup chopped onions
1 cup chopped celery
1 cup chopped carrots
2 cloves garlic, minced
2 tablespoons olive oil
2 ½ cups water
2 medium tomatoes, diced
1 (14.5 ounce) can peeled and diced tomatoes with juice
1 (10.75 ounce) can chicken broth
¼ cup uncooked barley
¼ teaspoon ground black pepper

DIRECTIONS:
In a large saucepan over medium heat, combine the onions, celery, carrots, garlic and oil and sauté for 5 to 10 minutes, or until all vegetables are almost tender. Add the water, fresh tomatoes, canned tomatoes, chicken broth, barley and ground black pepper.
Stir thoroughly and bring to a boil. Reduce heat to low and simmer for about 40 minutes until barley is tender.

NUTRITIONAL INFORMATION:
Servings: 6
Calories: 124
Total Fat: 5 g (36 %)
Total Carbohydrates: 18 g (55 %)
Dietary Fiber: 4.5 g
Protein: 3.5 g (9 %)

NOTES:

Tomato-Basil Soup

INGREDIENTS:
4 cups chopped seeded peeled tomatoes
4 cups tomato juice
½ cup fresh basil leaves
1 cup fat-free chicken stock
¼ teaspoon sea salt
¼ teaspoon pepper
½ cup low-fat yogurt

DIRECTIONS:
Bring chopped tomatoes and juice to a boil in a large saucepan. Reduce heat and simmer uncovered for 30 minutes. Place tomato mixture and basil (leaving a few fresh leaves for garnish) in a blender and process until smooth. Return pureed mixture to pan, add chicken stock, salt and pepper. Add yogurt, stirring with a whisk. Cook over medium heat until thick, about 5 minutes. Serve soup with additional fresh basil leaves.

NUTRITIONAL INFORMATION
Servings: 8 (1 cup)
Calories: 52
Total Fat: 0.5 g (11 %)
Total Carbohydrates: 10.5 g (74 %)
Dietary Fiber: 1.5 g
Protein: 3 g (17 %)

NOTES:

COLD SOUPS

Cantaloupe Soup with Basil and Crab

INGREDIENTS:
2 cups cubed cantaloupe
½ cup mango nectar
1 green onion, minced
6 basil leaves, shredded
Hot pepper sauce
¼ teaspoon salt
6 ounces cooked lump crab meat

DIRECTIONS:
Puree the cantaloupe with 1/2 cup mango nectar.
Pour the mixture into a large bowl and stir in the minced green onion, basil leaves, 3 dashes hot pepper sauce and salt.
Chill at least 2 hours. Top each serving with 3 ounces cooked lump crab meat.

NUTRITIONAL INFORMATION:
Servings: 2
Calories: 178
Total Fat: 2 g (10 %)
Total Carbohydrates: 23 g (47%)
Dietary Fiber: 2 g
Protein: 18.5 g (43 %)

NOTES:

INGREDIENTS:
1 chilled English cucumber
1 avocado
3 green onions, chopped
¼ cup mint leaves, chopped (optional)
½ cup nonfat buttermilk
1 ½ cups cold water
Salt and pepper to taste

DIRECTIONS:
Cut cucumber into 3 equal pieces, then coarsely chop 2 of the cucumber pieces. Coarsely chop half of the avocado. Blend together the chopped cucumber and avocado and the mint leaves, green onions, buttermilk and water until smooth. Season to taste with salt and pepper.
Chill soup, uncovered, 15 minutes. Cut remaining cucumber and avocado in ¼-inch pieces and stir into soup.

NUTRITIONAL INFORMATION:
Servings: 4
Calories: 97
Total Fat: 7 g (61 %)
Total Carbohydrates: 8 g (29 %)
Dietary Fiber: 4 g
Protein: 2.5 g (9%)

NOTES:

INGREDIENTS:
3 cups diced cantaloupe or honeydew melon
½ cup peach or apricot nectar
½ cup fat-free vanilla yogurt
½ teaspoon vanilla extract
1 cup diced, peeled and pitted peaches or plums
1 cup fresh blueberries
1 cup quartered strawberries or fresh raspberries

DIRECTIONS:
Process cantaloupe, nectar, yogurt and vanilla in a blender until smooth. Combine the mixture with the other fruits. Cover and refrigerate at least 2 hours.

NUTRITIONAL INFORMATION:
Servings: 5 (1 cup each)
Calories: 105
Fat: 1 g (6 %)
Carbohydrates: 23.5 g (84 %)
Dietary Fiber: 3 g
Protein: 3 g (11 %)

NOTES:

INGREDIENTS:
2 long, seedless cucumbers, halved but not peeled
3 red bell peppers, cored and seeded
8 plum tomatoes
2 red onions
6 garlic cloves, minced
64 ounces tomato juice
1 bunch of parsley
½ cup white wine vinegar
2 tablespoons olive oil
1 tablespoon kosher salt
1 ½ teaspoon freshly ground black pepper

DIRECTIONS:
Roughly chop vegetables. Put each vegetable separately in food processor fitted with steel blade and pulse until it is coarsely chopped. Do not over-process.
Combine veggies in large bowl and add garlic, tomato juice, vinegar, oil, salt and pepper. Mix well and chill before serving.

NUTRITIONAL INFORMATION:
Servings: 18 (1 cup)
Calories: 59
Total Fat: 2 g (27 %)
Total Carbohydrates: 11 g (65 %)
Dietary Fiber: 2 g
Protein: 2 g (8%)

NOTES: *This soup tastes better the longer you let it sit.*

Fish and Shellfish

*"One of the very nicest things about life is the way we must
regularly stop whatever it is we are doing
and devote our attention to eating."*
Pavarotti and Wright, Pavarotti, My Own Story

INGREDIENTS:
3 tablespoons brown sugar
3 tablespoons bourbon
2 tablespoons soy sauce
1 tablespoon grated peeled fresh ginger
1 tablespoon fresh lime juice
3 garlic cloves, minced
¼ teaspoon freshly ground black pepper
4 (6-ounce) skinless salmon fillets
Nonstick cooking spray
¼ cup thinly sliced green onions
1 tablespoon sesame seeds, toasted

DIRECTIONS:
Combine brown sugar, bourbon, soy sauce, ginger, lime juice and garlic in large plastic bag.
Add fish to bag and seal. Marinate in refrigerator 1 ½ hours, turning occasionally.
Heat a large nonstick skillet over medium-high heat. Coat pan with nonstick cooking spray,
add fish and marinade to pan; cook fish 4 minutes on each side or until fish flakes easily
when tested with a fork. When serving, drizzle each fillet with about 2 teaspoons sauce, and
sprinkle with 1 tablespoon green onions and ¼ teaspoon sesame seeds.

NUTRITIONAL INFORMATION:
Servings: 4
Calories: 353
Total Fat: 14 g (36 %)
Total Carbohydrates: 13 g (15 %)
Dietary Fiber: 5 g
Protein: 37.5 g (42 %)

NOTES:

INGREDIENTS:
½ teaspoon grated lime zest
3 tablespoons fresh lime juice
2 tablespoons soy sauce
⅛ teaspoon cayenne pepper
1 pound large shrimp, shelled and deveined
2 cups diced fresh pineapple
2 kiwifruits, peeled and diced
½ cup diced tart, crisp apple
1 tablespoon honey
2 tablespoons chopped parsley

DIRECTIONS:
In large bowl, stir together lime zest, 2 tablespoons lime juice, soy sauce and cayenne. Add the shrimp, tossing to coat, and let it marinade while you prepare the relish.
In large bowl, stir together pineapple, kiwifruit, apple, honey, parsley and remaining lime juice.
Preheat the broiler. Place the shrimp on broiler pan, drizzle the marinade over them and broil 5 inches from the heat for about 5 minutes, or until shrimp are just cooked through and browned.
Spoon relish onto plates and place the shrimp on top.

NUTRITIONAL INFORMATION:
Servings: 4
Calories: 140
Total Fat: 2 g (10 %)
Total Carbohydrates: 24 g (45 %0
Dietary Fiber: 3 g
Protein: 20 g (44 %)

NOTES:

INGREDIENTS:
¼ cup fine dry whole wheat bread crumbs
2 tablespoons grated Parmesan cheese
1 tablespoon cornmeal
1 teaspoon olive oil
½ teaspoon Italian seasoning
¼ teaspoon garlic powder
⅛ teaspoon ground black pepper
4 (4 ounce) cod fillets
1 egg white, lightly beaten

DIRECTIONS:
Preheat oven to 450 degrees F.
In a small shallow bowl, stir together the bread crumbs, cheese, cornmeal, oil, Italian seasoning, garlic powder and pepper; set aside. Coat the rack of a broiling pan with cooking spray. Place the cod on the rack, folding under any thin edges of the filets. Brush with the egg white, then spoon the crumb mixture evenly on top. Bake in a preheated oven for 10 to 12 minutes or until the fish flakes easily when tested with a fork and is opaque all the way through.

NUTRITIONAL INFORMATION:
Servings: 4
Calories: 254
Total Fat: 12 g (43 %)
Total Carbohydrates: 14 g (23 %)
Dietary Fiber: 0.5 g
Protein: 20.5 g (34 %)

NOTES:

Submitted by Paula Daskivich

INGREDIENTS:
1 tablespoon olive oil
2 garlic cloves, minced
½ onion, chopped
1 zucchini, chopped
1 large carrot, chopped
2 celery stalks, chopped
1 tablespoon gingerroot, chopped
½ jalapeno pepper, chopped
1 28-ounce can diced tomatoes, not drained
1 tablespoon cumin
½ tablespoon coriander
1 tablespoon dried oregano
½ teaspoon ground black pepper
7 ounces white fish fillet, chopped
7 ounces scallops, cut in half
1 ½ cups water

DIRECTIONS:
Heat oil in large pot over medium heat. Cook garlic and onion until soft. Add zucchini, carrot, celery, ginger and jalapeno pepper. Sauté for 5 minutes. Add tomatoes and juice, spices, fish, scallops and water. Bring to a boil. Reduce heat and simmer for 7-10 minutes.

NUTRITIONAL INFORMATION:
Servings: 4
Calories: 209
Total Fat: 5 g (22 %)
Total Carbohydrates: 21 g (31 %)
Dietary Fiber: 5 g
Protein: 21 g (40 %)

NOTES:

INGREDIENTS:
Nonstick cooking spray
4 tablespoons finely minced green onions
4 (6-ounce) flounder fillets
¾ teaspoon salt
⅛ teaspoon freshly ground white pepper
¼ cup pine nuts, lightly toasted and chopped
1 teaspoon finely grated lemon rind
⅓ cup dry white wine
Chopped parsley and lemon wedges (optional)

DIRECTIONS:
Preheat oven to 375 degrees F. Lightly coat the bottom of a 13x9-inch baking dish with cooking spray; sprinkle evenly with green onions.
Arrange fish in an even layer over the green onions, slightly overlapping if necessary.
Sprinkle with salt and pepper. Combine pine nuts and rind and sprinkle evenly over fish.
Pour wine around fish, being careful not to dislodge topping. Bake for 15 minutes or until fish flakes easily when tested with a fork or until desired degree of doneness. Garnish with parsley and lemon wedges if desired.

NUTRITIONAL INFORMATION:
Servings: 4 (1 fillet)
Calories: 204
Fat: 6 (27 %)g
Carbohydrates: 2 g (3 %)
Dietary Fiber: 0.5 g
Protein: 34 g (70 %)

NOTES:

INGREDIENTS:
4 tuna steaks, about 1 lb.
½ cup NEWAY™ approved teriyaki sauce
½ teaspoon garlic, minced
½ teaspoon fresh ginger, peeled and minced

DIRECTIONS: Mix the teriyaki sauce, ginger and garlic. Add the tuna and marinate in the refrigerator for at least 30 minutes, turning 2 or 3 times. Pre-heat the grill. Place the steaks on grill and cook until just done, basting with the marinade.

NUTRITIONAL INFORMATION:
Servings: 4
Calories: 148
Total Fat: 1 g (6%)
Total Carbohydrates: 5 g (14 %)
Dietary Fiber: 0 g
Protein: 28 g (81 %)

NOTES:

Lime-Baked Fish

INGREDIENTS:
½ pound fresh fish fillets
¼ cup fresh lime juice
1 teaspoon tarragon leaves
¼ cup chopped green onion tops
Nonstick cooking spray

DIRECTIONS:
Spray baking dish with nonstick cooking spray. Arrange the fish fillets in the baking dish and sprinkle with lime juice, tarragon and onion tops. Bake, covered, at 325 degrees for 15-20 minutes or until fish flakes easily.

NUTRITIONAL INFORMATION:
Servings: 2
Calories: 105
Total Fat: 1 g (10 %)
Total Carbohydrates: 3 g (8 %)
Dietary Fiber: 0.5 g
Protein: 20 g (82 %)

NOTES:

INGREDIENTS:
8 ounces fresh whole wheat linguine
1 tablespoon olive oil
¾ cup chopped red onion
3 cloves garlic, minced
½ teaspoon crushed red pepper
2 tablespoons tomato paste
1 (14.5-ounce) can diced tomatoes, undrained
2 (6.5-ounce) cans minced clams, undrained
2 tablespoons chopped fresh parsley
1 tablespoon chopped fresh basil
1 tablespoon chopped fresh oregano

DIRECTIONS;
Cook pasta according to package direction, omitting salt and fat. Drain.
Heat olive oil in a large nonstick skillet over medium-high heat. Add onion, garlic and crushed red pepper to pan; sauté 3 minutes or until onion is lightly browned. Stir in tomato paste and tomatoes; cook 4 minutes or until thick, stirring constantly. Stir in clams; cook 2 minutes or until thoroughly heated. Remove from heat and stir in parsley, basil and oregano. Serve with pasta.

NUTRITIONAL INFORMATION:
Servings: 4 (1 cup pasta and 1 cup sauce)
Calories: 321
Fat: 5 g (14 %)
Carbohydrates: 56 g (66 %)
Dietary Fiber: 3 g
Protein: 17.5 g (20 %)

NOTES:

Mustard Crusted Tilapia

INGREDIENTS:

2 (6 ounce) fresh tilapia fillets
1 teaspoon spicy brown mustard
1 teaspoon Worcestershire sauce
½ teaspoon lemon juice
¼ teaspoon garlic powder
¼ teaspoon dried oregano
1 tablespoon Parmesan cheese
1 tablespoon whole wheat seasoned bread crumbs
Nonstick cooking spray

DIRECTIONS:

Preheat oven to 375 degrees F and spray a glass baking dish with nonstick cooking spray. Place tilapia fillets into prepared baking dish, and bake in preheated oven for 10 minutes. Meanwhile, stir together the mustard, Worcestershire sauce, lemon juice, garlic powder, oregano, and Parmesan cheese. When fish has cooked for 10 minutes, spread with herb paste, and sprinkle with bread crumbs. Continue baking for another 5 minutes until the topping is bubbly and golden.

NUTRITIONAL INFORMATION:
Servings: 2
Calories: 168
Total Fat: 2.5 g (13 %)
Total Carbohydrates: 3 g (7 %)
Dietary Fiber: 0 g
Protein: 31.5 g (80 %)

NOTES:

INGREDIENTS:
12 ounces thick white fish fillet, cut in half
1 medium potato, about 5 ounces
Salt and freshly ground black pepper
¼ teaspoon dried rosemary leaves, crushed
1 tablespoon olive oil

DIRECTIONS:
Rinse the fish under cold running water and pat dry. Sprinkle with salt and pepper to taste. Peel potato and grate on large holes of a grater. Squeeze excess water out of potato by pressing between sheets of paper towel. Season the potato with salt, pepper and rosemary and press it around the fish. Heat a nonstick frying pan over medium-high heat and add olive oil. Gently slide the fish into the pan. Cook for 3 to 5 minutes. Turn fish over, using two spatulas, and cook for 3 to 5 minutes more or until potatoes are golden and fish is done.

NUTRITIONAL INFORMATION:
Servings: 2
Calories: 262
Total Fat: 8.5 g (28 %)
Total Carbohydrates: 14 g (22 %)
Dietary Fiber: 0.5 g
Protein: 31 g (50 %)

NOTES:

Scallops Skewers

INGREDIENTS:
20 sea scallops
1 cup cubed red pepper
½ cup cubed onion
2 cups mushrooms
¼ cup NEWAY™ approved teriyaki marinade
⅛ teaspoon ground ginger
4 large skewers

DIRECTIONS:
Place teriyaki marinade and ginger in a small bowl and mix well. Place scallops and vegetable pieces on skewers until you have 5 scallops and choice of vegetables on the skewer. Place skewers in a deep pan and drizzle the teriyaki sauce over each one. Let stand in refrigerator for 10 minutes or more. Place on grill for 10-15 minutes or until tender and cooked through.

NUTRITIONAL INFORMATION:
Servings: 4
Calories: 109
Total Fat: 2 g (19 %)
Total Carbohydrates: 7.5 g (33%)
Dietary Fiber: 0.5 g
Protein: 12 g (52 %)

NOTES:

INGREDIENTS:
1 cup whole wheat couscous
1 ¼ cups fat free chicken broth
2 tablespoons olive oil, divided
1 tablespoon balsamic vinegar
1 red pepper, seeded and sliced
1 lb peeled or deveined medium shrimp, tails removed
1 can black beans (15 oz), rinsed and drained
1 can corn (11 oz), drained
¼ cup fresh basil, finely shredded

DIRECTIONS:
In a medium saucepan, boil chicken broth. Remove from heat and add couscous. Set aside. In a large skillet, heat 1 tablespoon oil over medium-high heat. Add pepper and cook for 5 minutes. Stir in shrimp and sauté 3 minutes, or until shrimp are opaque throughout. Stir in black beans and corn; cook just to heat through. In a large bowl, toss together couscous and shrimp-bean mixture with 1 tablespoon olive oil and 1 tablespoon balsamic vinegar.

NUTRITIONAL INFORMATION:
Servings: 6
Calories: 330
Total Fat: 7.5 g (20 %)
Total Carbohydrates: 41 g (50 %)
Dietary Fiber: 6.5 g
Protein: 24.5 g (30 %)

NOTES:

INGREDIENTS:
4 teaspoons olive oil, divided
1 ½ cups cut fresh green beans
1 ½ cups finely chopped onion
3 cups lightly packed chopped fresh spinach
1 cup sugar snap peas, trimmed and sliced crosswise
16 medium shrimp, peeled, deveined and halved lengthwise
¼ teaspoon salt
1 (14 ½-ounce) can fat-free chicken broth
1 ½ cups water
1 cup brown rice, uncooked
½ teaspoon salt
¼ teaspoon freshly ground pepper
⅓ cup freshly grated Romano cheese

DIRECTIONS:
Heat 2 teaspoons live oil in a large, heavy saucepan over medium-high heat. Add green beans, carrot and onion and sauté 10 minutes or until just tender. Add spinach and sugar snap peas, cover and cook 3 minutes. Stir in shrimp and ¼ teaspoon salt. Cover and cook 1 minute. Transfer mixture to a bowl and set aside.
In small saucepan, simmer broth and water but do not boil. Keep warm over low heat.
In large, clean saucepan, heat the remaining 2 teaspoons oil over medium-high heat and add the rice. Cook 2 minutes, stirring constantly. Pour in 1 ½ cups hot broth mixture, reduce heat to medium and cook until liquid is nearly absorbed, stirring occasionally, about 8-10 minutes. Add remaining broth mixture in three batches, stirring constantly until each portion of broth is absorbed before adding the next (about 35 minutes total cooking time). Stir in vegetable and shrimp mixture, ¼ teaspoon salt and pepper; cook 3 minutes or until hot. Stir in cheese. Serve immediately.

NUTRITIONAL INFORMATION:
Servings: 4 (1 ¼ cups)
Calories: 325
Fat: 8.5 g (23 %)
Carbohydrates: 48 g (60 %)
Dietary Fiber: 6 g
Protein: 15 g (18 %)

NOTES:

INGREDIENTS:
16 jumbo shrimp, in shells
3 cloves garlic, minced
1 tablespoon butter
¼ cup basil, fresh
1 tablespoon white balsamic vinegar
¼ teaspoon salt
Parsley (optional)

DIRECTIONS:
Thaw shrimp, if frozen. Rinse shrimp; pat dry with paper towels. Preheat broiler. Using a sharp paring knife, split each shrimp down the back through the shell almost all the way through the meaty portion, leaving the legs intact. Devein shrimp. Loosen shrimp from shell by running knife between shell and shrimp meat. Flatten shrimp with your hand or the flat side of blade. (Or remove shell, leaving tail intact and flatten with hand or knife blade.) Arrange the prepared shrimp, split sides up, in a single layer on a broiler pan. Meanwhile, in a small saucepan, cook garlic in hot butter until tender. Stir in basil, white balsamic vinegar, and salt. Brush shrimp with garlic mixture. Broil shrimp 3 to 4 inches from the heat for 5 to 8 minutes or just until the shrimp are opaque. Transfer shrimp to a platter. If desired, surround with parsley.

NUTRITIONAL INFORMATION:
Servings: 4
Calories: 98
Total Fat: 4 g (36 %)
Total Carbohydrates: 1.5 g (6 %)
Dietary Fiber: 0 g
Protein: 13.5 g (58 %)

NOTES:

INGREDIENTS:
1 slice bacon
½ teaspoon salt
½ teaspoon smoked paprika
¼ teaspoon black pepper
4 skinless halibut fillets (6-ounce each)
1 tablespoon minced garlic
1 6-ounce package fresh baby spinach

DIRECTIONS:
Cook bacon in large nonstick skillet until crisp. Remove bacon from pan and crumble. Set aside.
Combine salt, paprika and pepper. Sprinkle over fish. Add fish to drippings in pan, and cook for 3 minutes on each side or until fish flakes easily. Remove from pan and keep warm.
Add minced garlic to pan and cook 1 minute, stirring frequently. Stir in bacon. Add spinach to pan and cook for 1 minute or until spinach begins to wilt. Serve with fish.

NUTRITIONAL INFORMATION:
Servings: 4
Calories: 206
Total Fat: 5 g (20 %)
Total Carbohydrates: 2 g (4 %)
Dietary Fiber: 1 g
Protein: 37 g (37 %)

NOTES:

INGREDIENTS:
1 ½ pounds firm whitefish
1 tablespoon olive oil
½ cup finely chopped onion
1 (14-oz.) can drained diced tomatoes
½ cup kalamata olives, sliced lengthwise
2 tablespoons dry white wine
1 teaspoon dried basil
½ teaspoon garlic powder
¼ teaspoon dried thyme

DIRECTIONS:
Heat oven to 375 degrees. Place fish in a single layer in large baking dish coated with cooking spray. Bake 15 minutes. Meanwhile, heat oil in medium saucepan on medium heat. Add onion; cook and stir 5 minutes or until softened. Add tomatoes, olives, wine, basil, garlic powder and thyme; simmer 3 minutes. Spoon sauce over fish. Bake 5 more minutes or until fish is opaque throughout.

NUTRITIONAL INFORMATION:
Servings: 6
Calories: 158
Total Fat: 4.5 g (25 %)
Total Carbohydrates: 6.5 g (15 %)
Dietary Fiber: 2 g
Protein: 21 g (56 %)

NOTES:

Poultry

*"You don't have to cook fancy or complicated masterpieces—
just good food from fresh ingredients."*
Julia Child

INGREDIENTS:
4 skinless, boneless chicken breast halves (20 ounces)
2 cups salsa
2 teaspoons garlic powder
1 teaspoon ground cumin
1 teaspoon chili powder
Salt and freshly ground black pepper to taste
1 ½ cups corn
1 ½ cups cooked pinto beans

DIRECTIONS:
Place chicken and salsa in the slow cooker the night before you want to eat this chili.
Season with garlic powder, cumin, chili powder, salt, and pepper. Cook 6 to 8 hours on Low setting.
About 3 to 4 hours before you want to eat, shred the chicken with 2 forks. Return the meat to the pot, and continue cooking. Stir the corn and the pinto beans into the slow cooker.
Simmer until ready to serve.

NUTRITIONAL INFORMATION:
Servings: 6
Calories: 231
Total Fat: 6.5 g (26 %)
Total Carbohydrates: 21.5 g (35 %)
Dietary Fiber: 5 g
Protein: 22.5 g (39 %)

NOTES:

INGREDIENTS:
1 tablespoon olive oil
1 garlic clove, crushed
1 tablespoon sliced fresh ginger
1 chicken breast, sliced (8 ounces)
2 green onions
8 ounces fresh asparagus, sliced on the diagonal
2 tablespoons soy sauce
¼ cup water
1 ounce slivered almonds

DIRECTIONS:
Heat large frying pan over high heat. Add oil and swirl to coat. Add garlic, ginger and chicken. Stir-fry 1 to 2 minutes, until chicken turns color. Add green onions and asparagus and stir-fry for 2 more minutes. Reduce heat and simmer for 2 minutes. Stir in soy sauce and ¼ cup water. Cover and continue to simmer for 2 more minutes, then cook until chicken and vegetables are tender. Toss in almonds.

NUTRITIONAL INFORMATION:
Servings: 2
Calories: 315
Fat: 19.5 g (55 %)
Total Carbohydrates: 10 g (11 %)
Dietary Fiber: 4.5 g
Protein: 27 g (34 %)

NOTES:

Chicken Barley Chili
Submitted by Bonnie Myers

INGREDIENTS:
1 can (14.5 ounce) diced tomatoes, undrained
1 jar (16 ounce) NEWAY™ approved salsa
1 can (14.5 ounce) fat-free chicken broth
1 cup medium barley
4 cups water
1 tablespoon chili powder
1 teaspoon cumin
1 can (15 ounces) black beans, drained and rinsed
1 can (15 ½ ounce) corn, undrained
3 cups cooked chicken breast, cut into bite-sized pieces

DIRECTIONS:
In large saucepan, combine tomatoes, salsa, broth, barley, water, chili powder and cumin. Bring to a boil, then cover and reduce heat to low. Simmer for 40 minutes, stirring occasionally.
Add beans, corn and chicken. Increase heat to high until chili comes to a boil. Cover and reduce heat to low and simmer for another 5 minutes, or until barley is tender. If chili becomes too thick, add more water.

NUTRITIONAL INFORMATION:
Servings: 12 (1 cup)
Calories: 222
Total Fat: 5.5 g (22 %)
Total Carbohydrates: 29 g (41 %)
Dietary Fiber: 6 g
Protein: 16 g (29 %)

NOTES:

INGREDIENTS:
1 whole garlic head
⅓ cup (3 ounces) feta cheese seasoned with your choice of herbs
6 skinless boneless chicken breasts halves (30 ounces)
½ teaspoon kosher salt
½ teaspoon freshly ground pepper
2 teaspoons olive oil

DIRECTIONS:
Preheat oven to 350 degrees F. Remove white papery skin from garlic head (do not peel or separate) and wrap garlic in foil. Bake for 1 hour; cool 10 minutes. Separate cloves, squeeze extract garlic pulp and discard skins. Combine garlic pulp, herbs and cheese, stirring well; set aside.
Cut a horizontal slit through the thickest portion of each chicken breast half to form a pocket. Stuff about 4 teaspoons cheese mixture into each pocket and sprinkle chicken evenly on both sides with salt and pepper.
Heat oil in large ovenproof skillet over medium-high heat. Add chicken to pan and cook 3 minutes or until lightly browned. Turn chicken over and bake for 20 minutes. Let stand 5 minutes before serving.

NUTRITIONAL INFORMATION:
Servings: 6
Calories: 201
Fat: 10 g (46 %)
Total Carbohydrates: 1.5 g (3 %)
Dietary Fiber: 0 g
Protein: 24.5 g (51 %)

NOTES:

INGREDIENTS:
2 cups chopped tomato
½ cup minced red onion
⅓ cup finely chopped fresh basil
2 teaspoons olive oil
1 teaspoon kosher salt
6 skinless, boneless chicken breasts halves (30 ounces)
¼ teaspoon freshly ground black pepper
Nonstick cooking spray
1 ounce crumbled Gorgonzola cheese

DIRECTIONS:
Combine tomato, onion, basil, oil and ½ teaspoon salt in bowl. Let stand at room temperature.
Place each chicken breast between 2 sheets of plastic wrap and pound to 1-inch thickness. Sprinkle both sides of chicken with remaining ½ teaspoon salt and pepper.
Heat large nonstick skillet over medium-high heat. Coat pan with nonstick cooking spray. Add chicken breasts to pan, cook 4 minutes on each side or until chicken is browned and done.
Stir cheese into tomato mixture. Top each chicken breast half with about ⅓ cup salsa.

NUTRITIONAL INFORMATION:
Servings: 6
Calories: 194
Total Fat: 9 g (41 %)
Total Carbohydrates: 4 g (8 %)
Dietary Fiber: 1 g
Protein: 24 g (52 %)

NOTES:

INGREDIENTS:
1 tablespoon chopped fresh oregano
1 tablespoon olive oil
1 teaspoon chili powder
¾ teaspoon ground cumin
½ teaspoon salt
3 garlic cloves, minced
4 skinless, boneless chicken breast halves (20 ounces)
Nonstick cooking spray
2 cups cubed seeded watermelon
1 cup cubed peeled ripe mango
¼ cup finely chopped red onion
2 tablespoons chopped fresh cilantro
2 tablespoons finely chopped seeded jalapeno pepper
1 tablespoon fresh lime juice
¼ teaspoon salt

DIRECTIONS:
Combine oregano, olive oil, chili powder, cumin, salt and garlic in large plastic bag. Add chicken to bag and seal. Marinate in refrigerator up to 4 hours, turning bag occasionally. Prepare grill and place chicken on a grill rack coated with nonstick cooking spray. Grill 5 minutes on each side or until done. Combine watermelon and remaining ingredients, and serve with chicken.

NUTRITIONAL INFORMATION:
Servings: 4 (1 chicken breast and 1 cup salsa)
Calories: 265
Total Fat: 11 g (36 %)
Total Carbohydrates: 14.5 g (20 %)
Dietary Fiber: 1.5 g
Protein: 27.5 g (44 %)

NOTES:

Chicken Capri

INGREDIENTS:
1 cup fat-free ricotta cheese
½ teaspoon dried oregano
¼ teaspoon salt
¼ teaspoon freshly ground black pepper
4 boneless, skinless chicken breast halves (20 ounces)
½ teaspoon garlic powder
1 ½ tablespoons olive oil
1 cup crushed tomatoes
4 ounces low-fat mozzarella cheese

DIRECTIONS:
Preheat the oven to 350°F.
In a blender or food processor, combine the ricotta with the oregano, salt, and pepper. Process to blend. Rub the chicken with the garlic powder. Heat the oil in a large skillet over medium-high heat. Add the chicken and cook 12 minutes per side. Place the chicken breasts, side by side, in a large baking dish and allow to cool.
Spoon ¼ cup of the cheese mixture and ¼ cup tomatoes onto each chicken breast. Top each chicken breast with 1 slice mozzarella. Bake for 20 minutes, or until the juices run clear.

NUTRITIONAL INFORMATION:
Servings: 4
Calories: 363
Total Fat: 17 g (42 %)
Total Carbohydrates: 9 g (9 %)
Dietary Fiber: 1 g
Protein: 41 g (17 %)

NOTES:

INGREDIENTS:
1 ounce dried mushrooms
2 tablespoons olive oil, divided
1 pound skinless, boneless chicken thighs
Sea salt and freshly ground black pepper to taste
½ cup white wine
½ cup canned, chopped, Italian tomatoes
½ cup chopped onion
½ cup pearl barley
¾ cup chicken broth

DIRECTIONS:
Place the mushrooms in a microwave safe bowl and add 1 cup of water. Microwave for 1 minute and let stand for 5 minutes. Lift the mushrooms from the liquid and rinse them under cold water; strain the liquid through a fine sieve lined with a paper towel and reserve the liquid.
Heat 1 tablespoon of live oil in a large skillet over high heat. Season the chicken with salt and pepper and add it to the pan. Brown on all sides. Add the wine, letting it boil rapidly for a minute and then stir with a wooden spoon to remove any browned bits that may be stuck to the pan.   Add the mushrooms, reserved liquid and the tomatoes. Turn down the heat so that the mixture simmers slowly and place a lid, slightly ajar, over the skillet. Cook until the chicken is completely tender, about 25 minutes.
Heat 1 tablespoon of olive oil in a small oven-proof pot. Add the onion and cook until it becomes translucent, about 4 minutes.   Add the barley, a pinch of salt and freshly ground pepper. Stir to coat the barley evenly with oil. Cook for 4 minutes, then add the broth and bring to a boil over high heat. Lower the heat so that the broth is barely simmering, cover with foil and cook until the barley is tender, about 20 minutes.   Divide the barley among 4 bowls, spoon the chicken mixture over the top and serve.

NUTRITIONAL INFORMATION:
Servings: 4
Calories: 390
Total Fat: 19 g (44 %)
Total Carbohydrates: 26 g (26 %)
Dietary Fiber: 6 g
Protein: 24 g (25 %)

NOTES:

INGREDIENTS:
Nonstick cooking spray
1 teaspoon olive oil
½ pound boneless chicken breast, rinsed and dried
½ teaspoon salt
⅛ teaspoon pepper
1 teaspoon chili powder
½ cup canned garbanzo or navy beans, drained and rinsed
½ cup fat-free ricotta cheese
½ cup shredded low-fat Cheddar cheese
4 8-inch whole-wheat tortillas
½ cup salsa

DIRECTIONS:
Preheat oven to 400 degrees F. Coat a large baking sheet with nonstick cooking spray.
Coat a large nonstick skillet with nonstick cooking spray and set it over medium-high heat.
When pan is hot, add oil. Sprinkle the chicken with salt, pepper and chili powder. Add it to
the pan and cook until no longer pink in the center, 4-5 minutes per side. Cut chicken into
thin slices.
In small bowl, mash beans with sour cream. Spread bean mixture over 2 of the tortillas in the
prepared baking sheet and arrange chicken slices on top. Spread cheese over the top and
press the other two tortillas on top to form a sandwich.
Bake until tortillas are crisp, 5-6 minutes. Cut into wedges and serve with salsa.

NUTRITIONAL INFORMATION:
Servings: 4
Calories: 281
Total Fat: 7.5 g (25 %)
Total Carbohydrates: 33 g (40 %)
Dietary Fiber: 7 g
Protein: 23 g (33 %)

NOTES:

Chicken with Wine

INGREDIENTS:
4 skinless chicken breasts, cut in strips (16 ounces)
2 egg whites, beaten
⅓ cup Parmesan
½ cup white wine
Sea salt and freshly ground black pepper to taste
2 tablespoons butter

DIRECTIONS:
Season chicken with salt and pepper. In shallow plate, spread cheese. Dip chicken in egg whites then coat with cheese.
In skillet, melt butter. Cook chicken until golden brown. Reduce heat, add wine and cover and simmer on low for 20 minutes.

NUTRITIONAL INFORMATION:
Servings: 4
Calories: 266
Total Fat: 14 g (46 %)
Total Carbohydrates: 1 g (1 %)
Dietary Fiber: 0 g
Protein: 26.5 g (43 %)

NOTES:

INGREDIENTS:
12 ounces boneless, skinless chicken thighs
½ teaspoon salt
⅛ teaspoon pepper
¼ teaspoon crushed red pepper flakes
2 medium onions, chopped
4 cloves garlic, minced
1 (14 ounce) can seasoned diced tomatoes
2 tablespoons tomato paste
1 cup fat-free chicken broth
½ teaspoon dried thyme leaves
½ teaspoon dried oregano leaves
3 tablespoons lemon juice
6 ounces cooked shrimp
1 cup frozen artichoke hearts, thawed and chopped
2 cups hot cooked whole wheat pasta
½ cup crumbled feta cheese

DIRECTIONS:
Cut chicken into large chunks and sprinkle with salt and pepper to taste. Place onion and garlic in bottom of crock pot and top with chicken. Combine the diced tomatoes with their liquid, the tomato paste, chicken broth, thyme, oregano, and lemon juice in a medium bowl and mix well. Pour over chicken. Cover crock pot and cook on low for 6-8 hours until chicken is tender and thoroughly cooked.
Stir in shrimp, and chopped artichoke hearts. Cover and cook for 15-20 minutes longer until thoroughly heated. Serve over hot cooked pasta and sprinkle with feta cheese.

NUTRITIONAL INFORMATION:
Servings: 4
Calories: 427
Total Fat: 15 g (31 %)
Total Carbohydrates: 40 g (35 %)
Dietary Fiber: 9 g
Protein: 37 g (35 %)

NOTES:

INGREDIENTS:
1 teaspoon onion powder
1 teaspoon garlic powder
1 teaspoon oregano
1 teaspoon basil
¾ teaspoon black pepper
3 chicken breasts, halved, boned and skinned (12 ounces)
3 chicken thighs, halved, boned and skinned (12 ounces)
1 tablespoon olive oil
2 cups sliced mushrooms
1 ½ cups red bell pepper strips
1 ½ cups green bell pepper strips
1 cup thin-sliced onion
1 28-ounce can tomatoes
1 6-ounce can tomato paste
2 bay leaves
1 tablespoon balsamic vinegar

DIRECTIONS:
Mix onion powder, garlic powder, oregano, basil and black pepper. Dredge chicken in these spices and set aside.
Put one tablespoon olive oil in bottom of crock pot. Add mushrooms, peppers and onion. Add tomatoes, tomato paste, bay leaves and vinegar. Add spiced chicken and any remaining spice mixture. Cook on low 7-9 hours. Serve with brown rice and salad.

NUTRITIONAL INFORMATION:
Servings: 6
Calories: 269
Total Fat: 11.5 g (38 %)
Total Carbohydrates: 20 g (27 %)
Dietary Fiber: 4 g
Protein: 23.5 g (35 %)

NOTES:

NEWAY™ Chicken-Stuffed Red Pepper
Rich Croce

INGREDIENTS:
4 medium red bell peppers
8 ounces chicken breast
1 tablespoon olive oil
Salt and freshly ground black pepper to taste
1 tablespoon dried or fresh basil
½ cup diced onions
3 ounces feta cheese, divided
1 ½ cups cubed zucchini

DIRECTIONS:
Preheat oven to 350 degrees F.
Heat oil in nonstick pan. Rub chicken with basil and salt and pepper to taste. Cook in olive oil, 3 minutes on each side. Remove chicken from pan, and add cubed zucchini and onions to the juices in pan, cook 4 minutes until crisp-tender.
Dice chicken. Remove tops and seeds from red bell peppers and set aside. In large bowl, combine cubed chicken, onions, zucchini and feta cheese. Stuff red peppers with chicken mixture and top each pepper with its top.
Bake in preheated oven for 45 minutes.

NUTRITIONAL INFORMATION:
Servings: 4
Calories: 210
Total Fat: 11 g (49 %)
Total Carbohydrates: 11 g (20 %)
Dietary Fiber: 3 g
Protein: 15.5 g (31 %)

NOTES:

INGREDIENTS:
Turkey:
1 pound boneless turkey breast chops
3 tablespoons lemon juice
1 tablespoon olive oil
2 shallots, minced
1 tablespoon capers, drained
1 teaspoon Dijon mustard
Sweet Potato:
3 medium sweet potatoes, cooked
4 tablespoons orange juice
¼ cup golden raisins
½ teaspoon ground cinnamon
Salt and freshly ground pepper to taste

DIRECTIONS:
To make the turkey, preheat broiler. Place turkey in a shallow roasting pan. Combine remaining turkey ingredients and pour over the turkey. Broil 6" from heat source 12-15 minutes or until turkey is cooked through.
To prepare potatoes, scoop hot sweet potato pulp into bowl and add remaining sweet potato ingredients expect salt and pepper. Purée and season to taste. Serve with the turkey.

NUTRITIONAL INFORMATION:
Servings: 4
Calories: 309
Total Fat: 7 g (20 %)
Total Carbohydrates: 30 g (35 %)
Dietary Fiber: 3 g
Protein: 30 g (39 %)

NOTES:

Olive Chicken

INGREDIENTS:
8 skinless, boneless chicken breasts (40 ounces)
Salt to taste
2 tablespoons canola oil
4 cloves garlic, crushed
1 bay leaf
¼ teaspoon dried thyme
¼ teaspoon ground black pepper
4 medium tomatoes, peeled and quartered
20 pimento-stuffed green olives
1 ¼ cups dry white wine
1 ¼ cups chicken broth

DIRECTIONS:
Season chicken with salt. Heat oil in a large skillet over medium high heat; brown chicken in oil, about 5 minutes each side. Add garlic, bay leaf, thyme and pepper and mix well, then stir in tomatoes, olives, wine and broth. Reduce heat to low and simmer, uncovered, for 45 minutes or until chicken is cooked through and juices run clear. Remove garlic and bay leaf and serve.

NUTRITION INFORMATION:
Servings: 8
Calories: 252
Total Fat: 11.5 g (41 %)
Total Carbohydrates: 4 g (6 %)
Dietary Fiber: 1 g
Protein: 27.5g (46 %)

NOTES:

INGREDIENTS:
1 cup chopped fresh pineapple
2 tablespoons chopped fresh parsley
2 tablespoons finely chopped red onion
⅓ cup unsalted, dry-roasted peanuts
1 (1-ounce) slice whole wheat bread
½ teaspoon salt
¼ teaspoon freshly ground black pepper
4 chicken cutlets (16 ounces)
1 ½ teaspoons canola oil
Dash of red pepper sauce
Parsley sprigs

DIRECTIONS:
Combine pineapple, parsley and red onion in a small bowl, tossing well. Combine peanuts and bread slice in food processor and process until finely chopped. Add a dash of red pepper sauce. Sprinkle salt and pepper evenly over chicken and dredge chicken in breadcrumb mixture.
Heat oil in large nonstick skillet over medium-high heat. Add chicken to pan and cook 2 minutes on each side or until done. Serve chicken with pineapple mixture. Garnish with parsely sprigs.

NUTRITIONAL INFORMATION:
Servings: 4 (1 cutlet and ¼ cup salsa)
Calories: 258
Total Fat: 13 g (45 %0
Total Carbohydrates: 10.5 g (15 %)
Dietary Fiber: 2 g
Protein: 25 g (40 %)

NOTES:

INGREDIENTS:
16 ounces boneless chicken breast, cut into one-inch pieces
4 teaspoons sesame seeds
Salt and freshly ground black pepper to taste
1 tablespoon olive oil
3 cups cabbage, sliced thin
½ pound mushrooms, stemmed and sliced thin
1 medium red bell pepper, seeded and sliced thin
1 medium carrot, peeled and sliced thin
2 celery stalks, sliced thin
1 cup snow peas, stemmed
4 teaspoons white wine vinegar
4 teaspoons soy sauce
1 ½ teaspoons sesame oil
1 teaspoon ginger, grated

DIRECTIONS:
Coat chicken with sesame seeds and season with salt and pepper. Heat olive oil in a sauté pan to medium heat. Add chicken and cook for about 5 minutes. Add cabbage and cook for 3 minutes. Add remaining vegetables and cook for an additional five minutes.
In a bowl, combine vinegar, soy sauce, sesame oil and ginger. Add to chicken and vegetables and cook for one minute. Remove from heat and serve.

NUTRITIONAL INFORMATION:
Servings: 4
Calories: 252
Total Fat: 13 g (42 %)
Total Carbohydrates: 13 g (18 %)
Dietary Fiber: 5 g
Protein: 25.5 g (17 %)

_____

NOTES:

INGREDIENTS:
Nonstick cooking spray
6 ounces whole-wheat spaghetti (2 cups cooked)
½ pound lean ground turkey
1 large egg white
2 tablespoons grated Parmesan
1 tablespoon Italian seasonings
2 cloves garlic, minced
1 (14.5-ounce) can diced tomatoes
1 teaspoon chili powder
1 teaspoon cumin
1 cup fat-free cottage cheese
½ teaspoon salt
¼ teaspoon pepper
1 cup shredded part-skim mozzarella
1 cup chopped onions
1 cup chopped broccoli, cooked

Preheat oven to 350 degrees F. Coat a 9-inch pie plate with nonstick cooking spray.
Cook pasta according to package instructions.
In small bowl, mix ground turkey with onion, egg white, Parmesan, Italian seasonings and garlic.
In large bowl, stir cooked pasta, tomato sauce, chili and cumin powder, cottage cheese and salt and pepper. Spoon mixture into pie plate. Spread meat on top and sprinkle with mozzarella. Bake uncovered until center is firm and cheese is bubbly, about 25 to 30 minutes.

NUTRITIONAL INFORMATION:
Servings: 8
Calories: 200
Fat: 5.5 g (26 %)
Carbohydrates: 23.5 g (44 %)
Dietary Fiber: 1 g
Protein: 15 g (30 %)

NOTES:

INGREDIENTS:
1 cup fresh parsley, packed
4 tablespoons brown sugar, divided
6 tablespoons fresh lime juice, divided
2 tablespoons Thai red curry paste, divided
¼ teaspoon red pepper flakes
Salt to taste
2 pounds boneless skinless chicken breast, sliced into ¼" –thick strips
½ cup creamy peanut butter
½ cup water
¼ cup green onions, chopped
¼ cup soy sauce
2 tablespoons fresh ginger, chopped
3 garlic cloves, chopped
16 Boston or Bibb lettuce leaves
16 strips each red bell pepper and cucumber
Lime wedges
Nonstick cooking spray

DIRECTIONS:
Blend parsley, 2 tablespoons brown sugar, 2 tablespoons lime juice, 1 tablespoon curry paste, pepper flakes and salt in food processor until smooth. Pour over chicken, toss to coat and marinate 10 minutes.
Preheat broiler to high with rack 6" from element. Coat a broiler pan with nonstick cooking spray.
Process 2 tablespoons brown sugar, 4 tablespoons lime juice and 1 tablespoon curry paste with peanut butter, water, green onions, soy sauce, ginger and garlic in food processor until smooth. Transfer to a serving dish.
Place chicken in prepared broiler pan, and broil chicken in batches until browned and cooked through, 6 minutes.
To serve, wrap a lettuce leaf around 2 strips of chicken, then add bell pepper and cucumber. Drizzle with sauce and lime juice.

NUTRITIONAL INFORMATION:
Servings: 8
Calories: 134
Total Fat: 5 g (34 %)
Total Carbohydrates: 7.5 g (19 %)
Dietary Fiber: 1 g
Protein: 16 g (48 %)

NOTES:

INGREDIENTS
1 tablespoon canola oil
1 medium onion, peeled and chopped
1 medium green bell pepper, seeded and chopped
2 garlic cloves, finely chopped
¾ pound ground turkey breast
1 can (28 oz.) diced tomatoes
2 tablespoons tomato paste
1/4 cup NEWAY™ barbecue sauce (see recipe)
Salt and freshly ground black pepper
6 whole-wheat hamburger buns, grilled or toasted
6 thin onion slices, for garnish (optional)
Shredded lettuce, for garnish (optional)

DIRECTIONS
Heat the oil in a medium skillet over medium-high heat. Sauté the onion and pepper until translucent, about 4 minutes.
Add the garlic and sauté until the vegetables are soft, about 3 minutes. Add the turkey and cook, using a wooden spoon to
break it up and stirring until it loses its pink color, about 4 minutes. Add the tomatoes, tomato paste and barbecue sauce. Simmer vigorously until the mixture is thick, about 15 minutes, stirring occasionally. Season to taste with salt and pepper.
Place the bottom of each bun on a plate. Spoon over each equal amounts of the meat mixture. Top with the onion and some lettuce, if using. Cover with the top of the bun.

NUTRITION INFORMATION:
Servings: 6 (1 burger with bun)
Calories: 272
Total Fat: 9 g (44 %)
Total Carbohydrates: 39 g (53 %)
Dietary Fiber: 7 g
Protein: 15 g (21 %)

NOTES:

INGREDIENTS:
1 (6 ounces) can tomato paste
½ cup dry red wine
½ cup water
1 clove garlic, minced
½ teaspoon dried basil leaves
¼ teaspoon dried oregano leaves
¼ teaspoon salt
16 ounces ground turkey breast
½ cup oatmeal
1 egg
1 cup shredded zucchini

DIRECTIONS:
Preheat oven to 350 degrees F. Combine tomato paste, wine, water, garlic, basil, oregano and salt in small saucepan. Bring to a boil, then reduce heat to low and simmer, uncovered, for 15 minutes. Set aside.
Combine turkey, oatmeal, egg, zucchini and ½ cup of tomato mixture in a large bowl. Mix well. Shape into a loaf and place into an ungreased 8"x4" loaf pan.
Bake for 45 minutes. Discard any drippings. Pour ½ cup of remaining tomato mixture over the top of loaf and bake for an additional 15 minutes.
Place on a serving platter. Cool for 10 minutes before slicing. Serve with remaining tomato sauce on the side.

NUTRITIONAL INFORMATION:
Servings: 8
Calories: 131
Total Fat: 5 g (34 %)
Total Carbohydrates: 8 g (25 %)
Dietary Fiber: 1.5 g
Protein: 11 g (33 %)

NOTES:

INGREDIENTS:
Juice and zest of 2 lemons
2 tablespoons fresh rosemary
1 teaspoon sage
2 tablespoons Dijon mustard
½ cup water
2 cloves garlic, crushed
Salt and pepper to taste
1 boneless turkey breast, about 2 pounds

DIRECTIONS:
Mix all ingredients except turkey to make the marinade. Place turkey breast and marinade in a large plastic bag and place in a large bowl. Make sure all the turkey is coated. Refrigerate 4-6 hours or overnight. Place turkey and marinade in a crock pot. Cover and cook on low for 8 hours or until tender.

NUTRITIONAL INFORMATION:
Servings: 8
Calories: 133
Total Fat: 1 g (7 %)
Total Carbohydrates: 2 g (6 %)
Dietary Fiber: 0 g
Protein: 28 g (84 %)

NOTES:

Meats

"He who distinguishes the true savor of his food can never be a glutton;
he who does not cannot be otherwise."
Henry David Thoreau

INGREDIENTS:
4 beef tenderloin steaks (16 ounces)
¼ teaspoon salt
¼ teaspoon freshly ground black pepper
Nonstick cooking spray
2 garlic cloves, minced
⅛ teaspoon crushed red pepper
3 tablespoons dry sherry
2 tablespoons soy sauce
2 tablespoons balsamic vinegar
2 teaspoons honey

DIRECTIONS:
Sprinkle both sides of steaks evenly with salt and black pepper. Heat a large nonstick skillet over medium-high heat. Coat pan with nonstick cooking spray. Add steaks to pan and cook 3 minutes on each side or until desired degree of doneness. Remove steaks from pan and keep warm.
Add garlic and red pepper to pan and sauté for 30 seconds; add sherry to pan and bring to a boil. Cook 30 seconds. Add soy sauce and remaining ingredients; bring to a boil, stirring occasionally. Reduce heat and cook 1 minute. Serve with steaks.

NUTRITIONAL INFORMATION:
Servings: 4 (1 steak and 1 tablespoon sauce)
Calories: 215
Total Fat: 9 g (38 %)
Total Carbohydrates: 4.5 g (8 %)
Dietary Fiber: 0 g
Protein: 24 g (45 %)

NOTES:

INGREDIENTS:
1 ½ cups chopped red onion
1 cup chopped red bell pepper
8 ounces 95 % fat free ground beef
2 garlic cloves, minced
1 ½ teaspoons chili powder
2 teaspoons ground cumin
1 teaspoon raw sugar
½ teaspoon salt
½ teaspoon dried oregano
1 can (19-ounce) red kidney beans, drained
1 can (14- ounce) fat-free beef broth
1 12-ounce bottle of beer
1 tablespoon yellow cornmeal
1 tablespoon fresh lime juice

DIRECTIONS:
Combine onions, pepper, beef and garlic in a large Dutch oven over medium-high heat.
Cook 5 minutes or until beef is browned, stirring to crumble. Stir in chili powder, cumin,
sugar and salt. Cook 1 minute. Add oregano, beans, broth and beer to pan. Bring to a boil.
Reduce heat and simmer 15 minutes. Stir in cornmeal, cook 5 minutes. Stir in juice.

NUTRITIONAL INFORMATION:
Servings: 4 (1 ½ cups each)
Per Serving: 251 Calories
Total Fat: 4 g (13 %)
Total Carbohydrates: 29 g (46 %)
Dietary Fiber: 7 g
Protein: 20 g (17 %)

NOTES:

INGREDIENTS:
⅓ cup balsamic vinegar
1 tablespoon olive oil
2 tablespoons water
1 green onion, thinly sliced
2 tablespoons chopped fresh oregano (or 2 teaspoons dried oregano)
1 ½ teaspoons chopped fresh thyme (or ½ teaspoon dried thyme)
2 cloves garlic, minced
¾ teaspoon kosher salt
½ teaspoon freshly ground black pepper
1 ½ pounds beef tenderloin or boneless sirloin, cut into 1-inch cubes
8 ounces fresh mushrooms
12 cherry tomatoes

DIRECTIONS:
For marinade, combine vinegar, oil, water, green onion, oregano, thyme, garlic, ¾ teaspoon kosher salt, and ½ teaspoon pepper. Place meat in a self-sealing plastic bag set in a shallow dish. Pour half of the marinade over meat and seal bag; turn to coat meat. Marinate meat in the refrigerator for 30 minutes to 1 hour, turning bag occasionally.
Pour remaining marinade over vegetables and marinate at room temperature for 20 minutes. Drain meat and vegetables, discarding marinade.
On 12 10-inch skewers, alternately thread beef, mushrooms, and tomatoes, leaving a quarter-inch space between pieces.
Grill until desired doneness, turning kebabs once halfway through grilling, 8 to 12 minutes for medium-rare doneness or 12 to 15 minutes for medium doneness.

NUTRITIONAL INFORMATION:
Servings: 6 (2 skewers each)
Calories: 194
Total Fat: 6.5 g (38 %)
Total Carbohydrates: 4 g (7 %)
Dietary Fiber: 1 g
Protein: 25 g (55 %)

NOTES:

INGREDIENTS:
2 tablespoons soy sauce, reduced-sodium
1 tablespoon cornstarch
1 tablespoon vinegar, white
1 tablespoon ginger, fresh
¼ teaspoon crushed red pepper
2 cloves garlic, minced
12 ounces beef, top sirloin steak
5 cups broccoli
2 teaspoons olive oil
2 medium carrots
¾ cup fat free beef broth
4 green onions or ½ cup diced onion
4 cups cooked spaghetti squash

DIRECTIONS:
For marinade, combine soy sauce, cornstarch, vinegar, ginger, crushed red pepper, and garlic in medium bowl.
Trim fat from meat. Cut meat across the grain into 1/8-inch-thick slices. Add meat to marinade; toss to coat. Cover and marinate at room temperature for 10 minutes. Drain meat, discarding marinade.
Cut broccoli flowerets from stems and cut stems into 1/4-inch-thick slices.
In a large skillet, heat 1 teaspoon of the oil over medium-high heat. Add meat; cook and stir in hot oil for 2 to 3 minutes or until slightly pink in center. Remove meat from the skillet and add the remaining 1 teaspoon oil, the broccoli and carrots; cook and stir for 1 minute. Add beef broth and cook for 5 to 7 minutes or until vegetables are crisp-tender, stirring to scrape up any browned bits from bottom of the skillet. Return cooked meat and add the green onions to the skillet; heat through.
Serve over hot cooked spaghetti squash.

NUTRITIONAL INFORMATION
Servings: 4
Calories: 228
Total Fat: 10 g (41 %)
Total Carbohydrates: 17 g (27 %)
Dietary Fiber: 3.5 g
Protein: 18 g (33 %)

NOTES:

INGREDIENTS:
8 ounces fresh orange juice
2 tablespoons soy sauce
1 tablespoon apple cider vinegar
2 large cloves garlic, minced
1 tablespoon chopped fresh ginger
2 teaspoons crushed red pepper
2 teaspoons ground black pepper
1 teaspoon orange peel
1 pound bottom round, trimmed and cut into 1 ½ " cubes
1 large zucchini, sliced ½" thick
1 large yellow bell pepper, cut into 2" chunks
1 large red bell pepper, cut into 2" chunks

DIRECTIONS:
In a flat baking dish, whisk together orange juice, soy sauce, vinegar, garlic, ginger, red pepper, black pepper and orange peel. Place the beef, zucchini and red and yellow pepper in the dish, coating well with the marinade. Cover the dish with plastic wrap, marinade in the refrigerator for at least 2 hours.
Preheat the grill. Alternate beef and vegetables on four 10" skewers. Place kebabs over heat and grill each side for 4 to 5 minutes, or until cooked through.

NUTRITIONAL INFORMATION:
Servings: 4
Calories: 250
Total Fat: 8.5 g (34 %)
Total Carbohydrates: 13 g (24 %)
Dietary Fiber: 2.5 g
Protein: 27 g (17 %)

NOTES:

INGREDIENTS:
1 pound ground sirloin
12 cherry tomatoes
2 egg whites
¾ cup old-fashioned oats
½ cup skim milk
1 cup chopped onion
Salt and pepper to taste
½ teaspoon oregano
1 tablespoon parsley
Nonstick cooking spray

DIRECTIONS:
Preheat oven to 375 degrees F and spray baking dish with nonstick cooking spray.
In a bowl, combine everything except meat and tomatoes. Add mixture to meat. Form meat around each cherry tomato so it is hidden inside. Place meatballs in the baking dish and bake for 25-30 minutes.

NUTRITIONAL INFORMATION:
Servings: 12
Calories: 84
Total Fat: 2 g (22 %)
Total Carbohydrates: 6 g (28 %)
Dietary Fiber: 1 g
Protein: 12 g (50 %)

NOTES:

INGREDIENTS:
2 small peaches, diced (1 cup)
1 pint grape tomatoes, halved
½ cup diced red onion
¼ cup chopped fresh cilantro
2 tablespoons chopped jalapeno peppers (no seeds)
½ cup fresh corn
2 cloves chopped garlic
¼ cup lime juice
¼ cup red wine vinegar
1 teaspoon kosher salt
Freshly ground pepper
1 (4 pound) pork tenderloin (about 15 4-ounces pieces)
1 tablespoon olive oil

DIRECTIONS:
Mix all ingredients together except pork and let sit for at least 1 hour or overnight.
Trim any fat from the pork tenderloin. Season with additional salt and pepper and rub with olive oil.
Grill until tender, temperature inside the thickest part reaching 140 degrees F. Let cool and slice thinly. Serve slices with cold or room temperature with the peach salsa.

NUTRITIONAL INFORMATION:
Servings: 15
Calories: 172
Total Fat: 5 g (28 %)
Total Carbohydrates: 5 g (9 %)
Dietary Fiber: 1 g
Protein: 26 g (63 %)

NOTES:

INGREDIENTS:
1 pound pork tenderloin medallions
¼ cup whole wheat flour
½ teaspoon salt
¼ teaspoon pepper
1 tablespoon olive oil
1 tablespoon chopped fresh rosemary
1 clove garlic, minced
½ cup dry red wine
½ cup chicken stock
⅛ cup sliced kalamata olives
1 tablespoon minced lemon zest

DIRECTIONS:
Pound the meat to ¼ inch thickness.
In a shallow bowl, combine the flour, salt, and pepper. Dredge pork in flour to coat.
Heat 1 tablespoon olive oil in a skillet over medium-high heat. Cook pork in olive oil until browned, turning once. Transfer meat to a warmed plate. Reduce the heat to low, and add rosemary and garlic to the pan. Pour in wine, and bring to a boil. Boil until the liquid is thick. Pour in chicken stock, and boil until volume is reduced by half. Stir in olives and lemon zest. Pour sauce over the meat and serve.

NUTRITIONAL INFORMATION:
Servings: 4
Calories: 205
Total Fat: 7 g (29 %)
Total Carbohydrates: 6.5 g (12 %)
Dietary Fiber: 1 g
Protein: 25 g (51 %)

NOTES:

INGREDIENTS:
3 cups diced ham
2 cups dried lentils
2 cups each diced carrots and celery
1 cup onions, chopped
2 cloves garlic, minced
4 cups water
1 teaspoon dried oregano
2 cans chicken broth
¼ teaspoon each salt and pepper
9 ounces fresh baby spinach leaves
2 tablespoons lemon juice
Lemon slices for garnish (optional)
Garnish: lemon slices

DURECTIONS:
Mix ham, lentils, carrots, celery, onion, garlic, water, oregano, chicken broth, salt and pepper in a 3 1/2 qt. crock pot. Cover and cook on high 4 to 5 hours or on low 7-9 hours until lentils are tender. Stir in spinach leaves, cover and cook 5 minutes or until tender. Stir in lemon juice.

NUTRITIONAL INFORMATION:
Servings: 11 (1 cup)
Calories: 194
Total Fat: 3 g (14 %)
Total Carbohydrates: 25.5 g (52 %)
Dietary Fiber: 12.5 g
Protein: 17.5 g (34 %)

NOTES:

INGREDIENTS:
1 medium red onion, quartered
⅓ cup balsamic vinegar
¼ cup capers, drained
2 tablespoons chopped fresh oregano
3 cloves garlic, minced
1 ½ pounds flank steak
¼ teaspoon salt
¼ teaspoon coarsely ground black pepper

DIRECTIONS:
Sliver one quarter of the onion and set aside.
Chop the rest of the onion. Mix it in a bowl with vinegar, capers, oregano and garlic.
Combine ¼ cup of this mixture with the slivered onion and set aside.
Sprinkle both sides of the steak with salt and pepper; prick well with a fork. Combine the steak with remaining onion mixture and marinate for 1 hour or overnight.
Heat the grill or broiler, positioning the oven broiler rack so that the meat on the rack in the pan is 4" from heat source. Remove meat from the marinade and discard marinade. Place the meat on the grill over direct heat or on an oven rack set in the broiler pan, and grill or broil for 4-5 minutes per side for medium-rare. Let stand for 5 minutes before slicing.
Place meat on a platter and pour reserved onion mixture over steak.

NUTRITIONAL INFORMATION:
Servings: 6
Calories: 216
Total Fat: 12 g (51 %)
Total Carbohydrates: 3 g (5 %)
Dietary Fiber: 0.5 g
Protein: 22.5 g (45 %)

NOTES:

INGREDIENTS:
1 (3 pound) boneless pork loin roast, cut into 2" pieces
½ teaspoon salt
2 (4 ounce) cans diced green chili peppers
3 cloves garlic, crushed
¼ cup chipotle sauce
3 ¼ cups water, divided
1 ½ cups uncooked long grain brown rice
¼ cup fresh lime juice
¼ cup chopped cilantro

DIRECTIONS:
Place the roast in a crock pot and season with salt. Place chili peppers and garlic on top of roast. Pour in the chipotle sauce and ½ cup water. Cover, and cook 7 hours on Low.
In a pot, bring remaining 2 ¾ cups water and rice to a boil. Mix in the lime juice and cilantro. Reduce heat to low, cover, and simmer 40 minutes.
Remove roast from the crock pot, and use two forks to shred. Return pork to the crock pot and allow meat to sit 15 minutes to absorb some of the liquid.
Serve over the cooked rice.

NUTRITIONAL INFORMATION:
Servings: 12
Per Serving: 261 Calories
Total Fat: 10 g (34 %)
Total Carbohydrates: 21 g (31 %)
Dietary Fiber: 1 g
Protein: 20.5 g (31 %)

NOTES:

Pepper Steak in Crock Pot

INGREDIENTS
2 pounds beef sirloin, cut into 2 inch strips with most of the fat trimmed
Garlic powder to taste
3 tablespoons canola oil
¼ cup beef broth
1 tablespoon cornstarch
1 large onion, chopped
2 large green bell peppers, roughly chopped
1 (14.5 ounce) can stewed tomatoes, with liquid
3 tablespoons soy sauce
1 teaspoon raw sugar
1 teaspoon salt

DIRECTIONS:
Sprinkle strips of sirloin with garlic powder to taste. In a large skillet over medium heat, heat the vegetable oil and brown the seasoned beef strips. Transfer to a crock pot. Mix cornstarch in beef broth until dissolved, then pour into the crock pot with meat. Stir in onion, green peppers, stewed tomatoes, soy sauce, sugar, and salt. Cover, and cook on High for 3 to 4 hours, or on Low for 6 to 8 hours.

NUTRITIONAL INFORMATION:
Servings: 6
Calories: 346
Total Fat: 18 g (47 %)
Total Carbohydrates: 12 g (13 %)
Dietary Fiber: 2 g
Protein: 33 g (40 %)

NOTES:

101

INGREDIENTS:
4 lean boneless pork chops (5 ounces each), ¾" thick
½ teaspoon salt
½ teaspoon ground rubbed sage
¼ teaspoon ground black pepper
1 tablespoon olive oil
6 pitted prunes, chopped
2 tablespoons apple cider vinegar
¼ cup dry white wine
2 tablespoons chopped walnuts

DIRECTIONS:
Season pork with salt, sage and pepper.
Heat oil in skillet over medium-high heat. Add pork and cook until browned on the first side, for 4 to 5 minutes. Turn and cook until the second side is browned, about 1 minute. Reduce heat to low and pour off any fat in the skillet. Add prunes, vinegar and wine or cider. Cook, turning once or twice, until the juices run clear, about 12 to 15 minutes.
Transfer to plates and spoon prunes on pork. There should be about 2 tablespoons of juices left in pan. If more, cook over low to medium heat until reduces. Spoon over pork and sprinkle with walnuts.

NUTRITIONAL INFORMATION:
Servings: 4
Per Serving: 293 calories
Total Fat: 13 g (40 %)
Total Carbohydrates: 8 g (11 %)
Dietary Fiber: 1 g
Protein: 32 g (46 %)

NOTES:

INGREDIENTS
4 large cloves garlic, peeled
1 ½ teaspoons coarse salt
2 tablespoons olive oil
1 tablespoon whole black peppercorns
2 pounds pork tenderloin, cut into 1 inch medallions
2 medium red bell peppers, julienned
1 cup white wine
2 lemons

DIRECTIONS
With a large mortar and pestle, mash the garlic, coarse salt, 1 tablespoon olive oil, and peppercorns into a fine paste. Transfer to a large bowl. Flatten the pork medallions to 1/4 inch thick. Place the meat in the bowl with the garlic mixture, tossing to coat. Cover, and marinate 2 to 4 hours in the refrigerator.
Heat the remaining oil in a large skillet over high heat. Stir in the pork and remaining garlic mixture. Quickly brown pork on each side, about 1 minute each. Remove from heat, and set aside. Place red peppers into the skillet, and sauté 2 to 5 minutes, until tender but firm. Pour white wine into the skillet, and scrape up the browned bits. Reduce heat to low, return pork to skillet, and continue cooking 10 to 15 minutes, to an internal temperature of 180 degrees F. Slice 1 ½ lemons into thin rounds. Transfer the pork and pepper mixture to a serving platter. Squeeze juice of remaining ½ lemon over the pork and peppers, and garnish with the lemon rounds.

NUTRITION INFORMATION
Servings: 8
Calories: 217
Total Fat: 9.5 g (39 %)
Total Carbohydrates: 4 g (4 %)
Dietary Fiber: 2 g
Protein: 24 g (44 %)

NOTES:

INGREDIENTS:
1 ½ pounds extra lean (90 %) ground beef
1 teaspoon salt
¼ teaspoon pepper
1 teaspoon Worcestershire sauce
1 tablespoon minced onion
Nonstick cooking spray
2 tablespoons spelt flour
1 (4-ounce) can sliced mushrooms
1 cup fat-free broth

DIRECTIONS:
Mix ground beef with seasonings and onion and shape into patties. Spray skillet with nonstick cooking spray and brown meat. Cook to desired doneness and remove to a hot platter.
Pour off all but 2 tablespoons of fat. Blend in flour. Pour in undrained mushrooms and beef broth and let the gravy thicken. Spoon over patties and serve.

NUTRITIONAL INFORMATION:
Servings: 6
Calories: 218
Total Fat: 12 g (49 %)
Total Carbohydrates: 3 g (4 %)
Dietary Fiber: 1 g
Protein: 23.5 g (46 %)

NOTES:

INGREDIENTS:
2 pounds beef stew meat, all visible fat trimmed off
1 ½ cups water
2 cloves garlic, minced
2 tablespoons chili powder
1 tablespoon vinegar
2 teaspoons dried oregano, crushed
1 teaspoon salt
1 teaspoon ground cumin
⅛ teaspoon pepper
12 whole wheat 10" tortillas
4 cups shredded romaine lettuce

DIRECTIONS:
In medium saucepan, combine meat, vinegar, water, garlic, chili powder, oregano, salt, cumin and pepper. Bring to a boil. Cover and reduce heat. Simmer about 2 hours or until meat is very tender. Uncover and boil rapidly about 15 minutes or until water has almost evaporated. Watch closely and stir near end of cooking time so meat doesn't stick. Remove from heat. Using two forks, finely shred meat.
Stack tortillas in foil; heat in 350-degree oven for 15 minutes. Spoon about ¼ cup meat mixture and a handful of shredded lettuce onto each tortilla near one edge. Fold edge nearest filling up and over filling just until mixture is covered. Fold in the two sides, then roll up. Fasten with wooden pick if needed.
Garnish with lettuce.

NUTRITIONAL INFORMATION:
Servings: 12
Calories: 240
Total Fat: 10 g (37 %)
Total Carbohydrates: 25 g (39 %)
Dietary Fiber: 3 g
Protein: 15.5 g (24 %)

NOTES:

INGREDIENTS:
1 tablespoon chopped fresh thyme, divided
1 ¼ teaspoon salt
½ teaspoon freshly ground pepper
¼ teaspoon ground allspice
1 ¾ pounds beef tenderloin, trimmed
Nonstick cooking spray
2 ounces brandy
½ cup minced green onions
1 ½ cups fat-free beef broth

DIRECTIONS:
Combine 2 teaspoons thyme, salt, pepper and allspice in a small bowl. Rub mixture evenly over all sides of beef; wrap tightly in plastic wrap and refrigerate 24 hours.
Preheat oven to 400 degrees F. Heat a large nonstick skillet over medium-high heat and coat pan with cooking spray. Add beef to pan; cook for 5 minutes, turning to brown on all sides.
Transfer beef to a roasting rack coated with nonstick cooking spray; place rack in roasting pan and bake at 400 degrees F for 26 minutes or desired degree of doneness. Remove from oven, and let stand for 10 minutes before slicing.
Pour brandy into roasting pan, scraping pan to loosen browned bits; set aside.
Heat skillet over medium heat; coat skillet with cooking spray. Add green onions to skillet cook 4 minutes or until tender, stirring occasionally. Add brandy mixture, broth and remaining thyme to skillet, scraping pan to loosen browned bits; simmer until reduced to 1 cup, about 4 minutes.
Serve with beef.

NUTRITIONAL INFORMATION:
Servings:7 (3 ounces beef and 2 tablespoons jus)
Calories: 173
Total Fat: 4 g (21 %)
Total Carbohydrates: 5.5 g (13 %)
Dietary Fiber: 0 g
Protein: 22 g (54 %)

NOTES:

INGREDIENTS:
4 boneless rib pork chops (4 ounces each)
¼ cup lime juice
1 tablespoon chili powder
1 tablespoon olive oil
2 cloves garlic
2 teaspoons ground cumin
1 teaspoon ground cinnamon
½ teaspoon hot sauce
¼ teaspoon salt
1 mango and chili peppers (optional)

DIRECTIONS:
Place chops in a resealable plastic bag set in a shallow dish. For marinade, in a small bowl, stir together lime juice, chili powder, oil, garlic, cumin, cinnamon, hot pepper sauce, and salt; pour over chops. Seal bag; turn to coat chops. Marinate in the refrigerator for 4 to 24 hours, turning bag occasionally.
Drain chops, discarding marinade. Place chops on the rack of an uncovered grill directly over medium coals. Grill for 11 to 14 minutes or until pork juices run clear (160°F), turning once. If desired, garnish with mango and/or chili peppers.

NUTRITIONAL INFORMATION:
Servings: 4
Calories: 209
Total Fat: 11 g (46 %)
Total Carbohydrates: 1.5 g (2 %)
Dietary Fiber: 0 g
Protein: 25 g (51 %)

NOTES:

Zucchini Pizza
Submitted by Joan Lockhart

INGREDIENTS:
4 cups shredded zucchini
1 ½ cups shredded part-skim mozarella, divided
2 egg whites, slightly beaten
1 pound ground meat, 80 % lean
1 cup onion, chopped
2 cloves garlic, minced
1 (14 oounce) can diced tomatoes
1 teaspoon salt, divided
2 teaspoons oregano
⅓ cup grated Parmesan cheese
Nonstick cooking spray
Toppings of your choice: peppers, mushrooms, etc.

DIRECTIONS:
Preheat oven to 400 degrees F and spray a 10x15 jelly roll pan with nonstick cooking spray.
Shred zucchini and squeeze out any moisture. Mix it with ½ cup mozarella, ½ teaspoon salt
and egg whites. Press mixture into the pan and bake for 20 minutes.
Over medium heat, cook beef, garlic and onion until done and drain any fat. Stir in diced
tomatoes, oregano and salt. Spoon over zucchini; add toppings. Sprinkle with remaining
mozarella and the parmesan. Bake for 30 minutes or until bubbly.

NUTRITIONAL INFORMATION:
Servings: 12 (no toppings)
Calories: 175
Total Fat: 11 g (57 %)
Total Carbohydrates: 5.5 g (11 %)
Dietary Fiber: 1 g
Protein: 14 g (32 %)

NOTES:

Going Meatless

*"Food is so primal, so essential a part of our lives,
often the mere sharing of recipes with strangers
turns them into good friends."*
Jasmine Heiler

Bean and Veggie Burritos

INGREDIENTS
1 (15 ounce) can of black bean or pinto beans, drained and rinsed
½ cup salsa
1 cup frozen corn
1 teaspoon chili powder
1 dash hot sauce (more or less to taste)
6 whole wheat tortillas
½ cup low-fat cheddar cheese, shredded
Nonfat sour cream (optional)

DIRECTIONS:
Drain beans and place in a medium sized saucepan. Mash roughly with a fork leaving some of the beans whole. Add corn, salsa, chili powder, and hot sauce. Mix well. Heat on medium until bean mixture is hot. Wrap tortillas in microwave safe plastic wrap and microwave on high for 40 seconds. Spoon bean mixture down center of each tortilla. Sprinkle with cheese. Top with sour cream. Roll up tortilla and serve.

NUTRITION INFORMATION:
Servings: 6
Calories: 219
Total Fat: 4.5 g (18 %)
Total Carbohydrates: 40 g (60 %)
Dietary Fiber: 11 g
Protein: 12.5 g (20 %)

NOTES:

INGREDIENTS:
2 medium ears sweet corn, husks removed (1 cup)
2 medium yellow summer squash, halved lengthwise
1 medium sweet onion, cut into ¼-inch slices
1 jalapeno pepper
1 tablespoon minced fresh basil
1 ½ teaspoons minced fresh oregano
1 garlic clove, minced
¼ teaspoon salt
¼ teaspoon ground cumin
6 whole wheat tortillas (8")
1 cup shredded low-fat Monterey Jack Cheese
1 tablespoon olive oil

DIRECTIONS:
Grill corn, covered, over medium heat for 10 minutes; turn. Place squash, onion and jalapenos on grill, cover and cook for 10 minutes, turning once. When vegetables are cool enough to handle, remove corn from the cobs, chop squash and onion, and seed and chop jalapenos. Place in large bowl. Stir in spices.
Place ½ cup filling on one side of each tortilla. Sprinkle with cheese, Fold tortillas over filling. On a griddle or large skillet, cook quesadillas in oil over medium heat for 1-2 minutes on each side or until heated through. Cut into wedges.

NUTRITIONAL INFORMATION:
Servings: 6
Calories: 242
Total Fat: 10 g (36 %)
Total Carbohydrates: 34 g (46 %)
Dietary Fiber: 7.5 g
Protein: 7.5 g (16 %)

NOTES:

INGREDIENTS:
2 eggplants (2 pounds), peeled and sliced lengthwise into ¼"-thick slabs
3 tablespoons olive oil
½ teaspoon salt
1 can (15 ½ ounces) crushed or chopped tomatoes
1 tablespoon and 1 ½ teaspoons tomato paste
1 teaspoon dried basil or 3 large fresh leaves, chopped
½ teaspoon dried rosemary, crumbled
¼ teaspoon ground black pepper
1 cup shredded mozzarella
½ cup grated Parmesan cheese

DIRECTIONS;
Preheat broiler.
Place eggplants on a large baking sheet and brush both side of each with the oil. Sprinkle with ¼ teaspoon salt.
Broil 5" from the heat, until just beginning to brown, for 2 to 3 minutes per side.
Set oven temperature to 375 degrees F.
In medium saucepan, combine tomatoes with juice, tomato paste, basil and rosemary. Cook over medium-low heat, stirring occasionally, until slightly thickened, for about 15 minutes. Season with the remaining ¼ teaspoon salt and the pepper.
Spread a layer of tomato mixture over the bottom of a 1 ½-quart baking dish. Add a layer of eggplant and top with another layer of tomato mixture. Sprinkle with a thin layer of mozzarella and Parmesan. Continue making 2 more layers with the remaining eggplant, tomato mixture and cheese, ending with a thick layer of cheeses. Bake until bubbling, for 25 to 30 minutes. Let stand for 10 minutes before cutting.

NUTRITIONAL INFORMATION:
Servings: 6
Calories: 224
Total Fat: 14 g (56 %)
Total Carbohydrates: 16 g (20 %)
Dietary Fiber: 5 g
Protein: 11 g (20 %)

NOTES:

INGREDIENTS:
2 large whole wheat flour tortillas
1 tablespoon olive oil
2 ounces feta cheese, crumbled
½ cup pitted and sliced olives
2 cups spinach leaves
½ cup red onion rings

DIRECTIONS:
Preheat over to 425 Fahrenheit. Lightly brush tortillas with olive oil, place on baking sheet and bake until tortilla begins to crisp, about 2 minutes. Turn tortilla over and brush with more olive oil, sprinkle half the feta, onion rings and 2 tablespoons olives over each. Bake for 3 to 5 minutes.
Scatter spinach on top and drizzle with remaining olive oil. Return to oven and bake for 1-2 minutes, until heated through.

NUTRITIONAL INFORMATION:
Servings: 2
Calories: 300
Total Fat: 19.5 g (58 %)
Total Carbohydrates: 27 g (29%)
Dietary Fiber: 6.5 g
Protein: 9.5 g (13 %)

NOTES:

INGREDIENTS:
8 ounces whole wheat fettuccini
1 tablespoon olive oil
¾ cup evaporated skim milk
⅓ cup grated Parmesan (1 ½ ounces)
¼ cup sliced green onion
2 tablespoons snipped fresh basil, or ½ teaspoon dried basil, crushed
¼ teaspoon finely shredded lemon peel
¼ teaspoon garlic powder
⅛ teaspoon pepper
Grated Parmesan (optional)
Quartered lemon slices (optional)

DIRECTIONS:
Cook pasta according to package directions. Drain. Immediately return pasta to pan and add olive oil. Toss to coat. Add milk, ⅓ cup Parmesan cheese, green onion, basil, lemon peel, garlic powder and pepper.
Cook over medium-high heat till bubbly, stirring constantly. Season to taste. Top with additional Parmesan cheese and fresh basil if desired.
Serve with lemon if desired.

NUTRITIONAL INFORMATION:
Servings: 6 side dishes
Calories: 213
Total Fat: 4 g (17 %)
Total Carbohydrates: 33 g (60 %)
Dietary Fiber: 1 g
Protein: 10 g (19 %)

NOTES:

Janie's Hummus Pizza
Janie McKirgan

INGREDIENTS:
1 large whole wheat pita (6 ½ to 7")
1 ½ tablespoons hummus
¼ cup grape tomatoes, chopped
2 sliced mushrooms
1 cup spinach leaves
Few slivers of red onion
1 tablespoon feta cheese, crumbled

DIRECTIONS:
Preheat oven to 425 degrees F. Spread hummus on pita. Pile on veggies and sprinkle with crumbled feta. Bake in preheated oven for about 10 minutes.

NUTRITIONAL INFORMATION:
Servings:1
Calories: 307
Total Fat: 7 g (21 %)
Total Carbohydrates: 53 g (59 %)
Dietary Fiber: 8g
Protein: 12 g (16 %)

NOTES:

Kathy's Vegetarian Chili
Submitted by Kathy Sell

INGREDIENTS:
1 tablespoon olive oil
3 cloves garlic, minced
1 cup chopped onion
1 cup chopped carrots
1 cup chopped green bell pepper
1 cup chopped red bell pepper
2 tablespoons chili powder
1 ½ cups chopped fresh mushrooms
1 (28 ounce) can diced peeled tomatoes with liquid
1 (15 ounce) can black beans
1 (15 ounce) can kidney beans
1 (15 ounce) can pinto beans
1 (15 ounce) can whole kernel corn, drained
1 tablespoon cumin
1 ½ tablespoons dried oregano
1 ½ tablespoons dried basil
½ tablespoon garlic powder

DIRECTIONS:
Heat oil in large pot over medium heat. Cook and stir in garlic, onion and carrots until tender. Mix in green and red bell pepper, season with chili powder. Continue cooking 5 minutes or until peppers are tender. Mix mushrooms into the pot and stir in tomatoes with liquid, all the beans with liquid and the corn. Season with cumin, oregano, basil and garlic powder. Bring to a boil, reduce heat to low. Cover and cook about one hour.

NUTRITIONAL INFORMATION:
Servings: 16 (1/2 cup)
Calories: 114
Total Fat: 2 g (15 %)
Total Carbohydrates: 20.5 g (70 %)
Dietary Fiber: 6 g
Protein: 3.5 g (15 %)

NOTES:

INGREDIENTS:
1 10 ounces package frozen chopped spinach
2 eggs
5 egg whites
¾ cup reduced-fat shredded Cheddar cheese
⅓ cup diced green bell peppers
⅓ cup diced onions
1 teaspoon Italian seasonings
3 drops hot-pepper sauce (optional)
Nonstick cooking spray

DIRECTIONS:
Microwave spinach for 2 ½ minutes on high. Drain excess liquid.
Preheat oven to 350 degrees F and spray muffin cups with nonstick cooking spray.
Combine eggs, cheese, peppers, onions, Italian seasonings and spinach in a bowl. Mix well.
Divide evenly among muffin cups. Bake for 20 minutes, or until knife inserted in the center
comes out clean.

NUTRITIONAL INFORMATION:
Servings: 6
Calories: 80
Total Fat: 3 g (31 %)
Total Carbohydrates: 4 g (19 %)
Dietary Fiber: 1 g
Protein: 10 g (50 %)

NOTES:

INGREDIENTS:
4 large Portabella mushrooms
2 cloves garlic, sliced into very thin slivers
1 teaspoon fresh rosemary (or 1/2 teaspoon dried)
1 teaspoon fresh thyme (or 1/2 teaspoon dried)
½ tablespoon olive oil
2 tablespoons balsamic vinegar
Salt and freshly ground black pepper

DIRECTIONS:
Preheat broiler or grill. Wipe mushrooms with damp cloth. Remove stems. With paring knife, make slits in tops of caps. Stuff slivers of garlic and herbs (if using) into slits. In small bowl, whisk together oil and vinegar with salt and pepper to taste. Brush mushrooms with oil mixture. Place mushrooms, cap-side down, on pan and broil or grill until soft and brown, about 3 to 5 minutes per side.

NUTRITION INFORMATION:
Servings: 4
Calories: 48
Total Fat: 2 g (35 %)
Total Carbohydrates: 7 g (48 %)
Dietary Fiber: 2 g
Protein: 3 g (16 %)

NOTES:

INGREDIENTS:
1 teaspoon canola oil
½ medium bell pepper, chopped
2 tablespoons chopped red onion
½ cup canned black beans, rinsed
2 tablespoons water
½ cup cooked quinoa

DIRECTIONS:
Heat oil in a small saucepan over medium heat. Add bell pepper and onion and cook until almost tender. Add beans and water to the pan. Cook until heated through. Stir in quinoa.

NUTRITIONAL INFORMATION:
Servings: 2 (1/2 cup)
Calories: 162
Total Fat: 4 g (22 %)
Total Carbohydrates: 27 g (57 %)
Dietary Fiber: 4 g
Protein: 6 g (15 %)

NOTES: Stir in your favorite salsa for extra zing.

Spaghetti Squash Lasagna
Karen Stein

INGREDIENTS:
1 spaghetti squash, about 2 lbs.
1 medium green pepper, chopped
1 medium onion, chopped
1 teaspoon basil leaves, crushed
1 teaspoon oregano leaves, crushed
1 clove garlic minced
¼ teaspoon each of marjoram, thyme, and sage
2 tablespoons olive oil
2 (14.5 ounces) cans diced tomatoes
8 oz part-skim mozzarella cheese
7 oz whole wheat pasta
2 cups NEWAY™ marinara sauce (See Recipe)

DIRECTIONS:
Wash squash, prick with fork. Cook in 400 degree oven until tender, about 40 minutes.
Turn oven down to 350 degrees F and coat an 11x13" baking dish with nonstick cooking spray.
Cook and stir green pepper and onion with seasoning in oil over medium heat until vegetables are tender. Stir in tomatoes and the sauce. Simmer uncovered 5 minutes. Cut squash into halves, remove seeds and fibrous strings. Remove spaghetti-like squash strands with two forks. Prepare pasta as directed on package. Toss the vegetable mixture and the pasta together in a large bowl.
Put half of this mixture into the baking dish, sprinkle half the cheese over the mixture. Add the remaining vegetable-pasta mixture on top of the cheese and then cover the entire casserole with the remaining cheese.
Bake for about 40 minutes until heated through and the cheese is melted.

NUTRITIONAL INFORMATION:
Servings: 12
Calories: 234
Total Fat: 8.5 g (32 %)
Total Carbohydrates: 25.5 g (39 %)
Dietary Fiber: 2.5 g
Protein: 8 g (14 %)

NOTES:

INGREDIENTS:
½ cup frozen chopped spinach, thawed, drained and squeezed dry
½ cup cooked, shredded spaghetti squash
1 beaten egg
3 egg whites
1 (12 fluid ounce) can evaporated skim milk
1 cup part-skim mozzarella cheese
Salt, garlic powder, oregano and pepper to taste
Nonstick cooking spray
⅓ cup whole wheat bread crumbs

DIRECTIONS:
Preheat oven to 350 degrees F (175 degrees C). Pierce squash several times with a fork, and place in a microwave-safe dish. Microwave on high for 10 minutes, turn over, and continue cooking 10 minutes more. Squash flesh should be very tender inside. Set aside to cool.
Cut squash in half lengthwise and scoop out seeds. Shred 1/2 cup of squash and place in a mixing bowl. Stir in egg, egg whites, evaporated milk, mozzarella cheese, and spinach until well combined. Spray a 9 inch pie place or quiche dish with cooking spray. Spread bread crumbs in the bottom and around the sides to coat. Pour egg mixture into prepared dish. Bake quiche in the preheated oven for 45 minutes, or until a toothpick inserted in the center comes out clean. Allow to cool for at least 10 minutes before cutting.
Serve warm or at room temperature.

NUTRITIONAL INFORMATION:
Servings: 6
Calories: 130
Total Fat: 4.5 g (31 %)
Total Carbohydrates: 10.5 g (32 %)
Dietary Fiber: 1 g
Protein: 12 g (38 %)

NOTES:

INGREDIENTS:
2 7" whole wheat pitas
⅛ cup raisins
1 tablespoon balsamic vinegar
1 teaspoon olive oil
1 clove garlic, minced
Sea salt and freshly ground black pepper
⅛ cup feta cheese
½ cup fresh strawberries, washed, hulled and sliced
½ cup fresh mango (about 1/2 medium), peeled, seeded and cubed
½ cup fresh blueberries

DIRECTIONS:
Preheat oven to 350 F.
In small bowl, combine olive oil, balsamic vinegar, honey, garlic and salt/pepper. Set dressing aside.
Place tortilla on ungreased baking sheet. Brush crust with dressing. Sprinkle cheese on tortilla, bake 6 minutes until warm.
In large bowl, combine all remaining ingredients and toss them with remaining dressing. Place on tortilla. Slice and serve immediately.

NUTRITIONAL INFORMATION:
Servings: 2
Calories: 252
Total Fat: 4.5 g (18 %)
Total Carbohydrates: 45 g (62 %)
Dietary Fiber: 6 g
Protein: 8 g (13 %)

NOTES:

INGREDIENTS:
1 package active dry yeast
1 cup warm water
1 teaspoon salt
2 ½ cups whole-wheat flour
1 ½ cups homemade tomato sauce
1 cup low-fat shredded mozzarella
Nonstick cooking spray

DIRECTIONS:
In a large bowl dissolve yeast in warm water. Add in salt, olive oil and flour. Knead dough until smooth. Roll dough out onto floured was paper. Let dough rise for about 1 hour. Mold into round 12-inch pizza pan well coated with nonstick cooking spray. Spread tomato sauce over dough and sprinkle with cheese. Bake at 450 degrees F for 10-15 minutes.

NUTRITIONAL INFORMATION:
Servings: 8
Calories: 239
Fat: 6 g (22 %)
Carbohydrates: 34.5 g (53 %)
Dietary Fiber: 6 g
Protein: 14 g (23 %)

NOTES:

INGREDIENTS:
4 medium to large zucchini, halved
1 tablespoon olive oil
1 red onion, chopped
2 cloves garlic, crushed
8 ounce button mushrooms, sliced
2 teaspoons cumin
1 (15.5 oz) can chick peas, drained and rinsed
½ lemon, juiced
1 tablespoon chopped fresh parsley
Sea salt and freshly ground black pepper to taste
Nonstick cooking spray

DIRECTIONS:
Preheat oven to 350 degrees F. Spray a shallow baking dish with nonstick cooking spray.
Scoop out the flesh of the zucchini; chop the flesh and set aside. Place the shells in the prepared dish.
Heat oil in large skillet over medium heat. Sauté onions for 5 minutes, then add garlic and sauté 2 minutes more. Stir in chopped zucchini and mushrooms, sauté 5 minutes. Sir in coriander, cumin, chick peas, lemon juice, salt and pepper. Spoon mixture into zucchini shells.
Bake in preheated over for 40 minutes, or until zucchini are tender.

NUTRITIONAL INFORMATION:
Servings: 8
Calories: 107
Total Fat: 2.5 g (21 %)
Total Carbohydrates: 18.5 g (52 %)
Dietary Fiber: 4.5 g
Protein: 5.5 g (21 %)

NOTES:

Salads, Both Light and Serious, and Dressings Too

"It's difficult to think anything but pleasant thoughts while eating a homegrown tomato."
Lewis Grizzard

Light Salad (Starters and Side Dishes)

Apple, Grape and Walnut Salad

INGREDIENTS:
¼ cup walnut halves
2 celery stalks, thinly sliced on the diagonal
1 large Granny Smith apple, cored, halved and thinly sliced
1 cup seedless red grapes, halved
1 tablespoon red wine vinegar
1 tablespoon olive oil
Coarse salt and freshly ground pepper

DIRECTIONS:
Preheat oven to 350. Spread walnuts on a rimmed baking sheet, and bake until lightly browned, 4-6 minutes.
In a large bowl, combine celery, apple, grapes, walnuts, vinegar and oil. Season with salt and pepper and toss to combine.

NUTRITIONAL INFORMATION:
Servings: 4 (1 cup)
Per Serving: 142 Calories
Total Fat : 9 g (53 %)
Total Carbohydrates: 14 g (37 %)
Dietary Fiber: 3 g
Protein: 2 g (7 %)

NOTES:

Apple Spinach Salad
Submitted by Jamie Okopal

INGREDIENTS:
2 tablespoons fresh orange juice
2 tablespoons fresh lime juice
2 teaspoons Dijon mustard
2 teaspoons honey
¼ teaspoon salt
⅛ teaspoon black pepper
½ cup thinly sliced red onion
1 large, firm, sweet-tart apple cored and thinly sliced
¼ cup crumbled blue cheese
1 cup diced strawberries
10 oz. fresh spinach

DIRECTIONS:
Combine juices, mustard, honey, salt and pepper in bowl and whisk together.
Combine remaining ingredients except the cheese; drizzle with dressing.
Toss to coat and sprinkle with cheese.

NUTRITIONAL INFORMATION:
Servings: 6
Calories: 74
Total Fat: 2 g (24 %)
Total Carbohydrates: 13 g (64 %0
Dietary Fiber: 3 g
Protein: 3 g (15 %)

NOTES:

Avocado and Grapefruit Salad

INGREDIENTS:
8 cups lettuce, mixed greens or spinach leaves
2 grapefruits
1 avocado
2 tablespoons raspberry vinegar
2 tablespoons olive oil
1 clove garlic, minced
½ cup red onion slivers
1 tablespoon water
1 teaspoon raw sugar
⅛ teaspoon salt

DIRECTIONS:
On a large serving platter, arrange the mixed salad greens and/or spinach, grapefruit sections, onion slivers and avocado slices.
In a small bowl, whisk together raspberry vinegar, olive oil, garlic, water, sugar, and salt. Drizzle over the salad mixture.

NUTRITIONAL INFORMATION:
Servings: 6
Calories: 130
Total Fat: 1 g (61 %)
Total Carbohydrates: 12.5 g (34 %)
Dietary Fiber: 4 g
Protein: 2.5 g (5 %)

NOTES:

Bean Salad

Submitted by Ann Marie Ober

INGREDIENTS:
4 cups green or yellow beans
1 cucumber, seeded and julienned
½ cup diced red onion
2 cloves garlic, minced
1 can kidney beans, drained and rinsed
1 tablespoon olive oil
1 tablespoon red wine vinegar
2 tablespoons Dijon mustard
¼ cup chopped fresh parsley
⅛ cup chopped fresh basil
Salt and freshly ground pepper to taste
1 teaspoon raw sugar

DIRECTIONS:
Cook beans in boiling water for 6 minutes. Put them directly in ice water to stop the cooking.
In a large bowl, mix together garlic, onion, oil, vinegar, mustard, parsley, basil, salt, pepper and raw sugar. Mix well.
Add green beans, kidney beans and cucumber to the bowl and mix well.

NUTRITIONAL INFORMATION:
Servings: 8 (1 cup)
Per serving: 92 Calories
Total Fat: 2.5 g (21 %)
Total Carbohydrates: 15 g (64 %)
Dietary Fiber: 5.5 g
Protein: 4 g (14 %)

NOTES:

Cauliflower Salad

INGREDIENTS:
1 medium head cauliflower, blanched for 5 minutes
1 (2-oz.) can anchovies, drained and chopped
1 tablespoon drained capers
2 tablespoons fresh lemon juice
1 tablespoon olive oil
1 garlic clove, minced
1 tablespoon chopped fresh oregano (or 1 teaspoon dried)

DIRECTIONS:
Drain cauliflower and break into small pieces. Combine cauliflower, anchovies and capers in medium bowl. Combine remaining ingredients and toss with cauliflower mixture.

NUTRITIONAL INFORMATION:
Servings: 4
Calories: 92
Total Fat: 5 g (46 %)
Total Carbohydrates: 8 g (32 %)
Dietary Fiber: 4 g
Protein: 6 g (23 %)

NOTES:

Chinese Green Bean Salad

INGREDIENTS:
1 pound fresh green beans
1 tablespoon finely chopped fresh ginger root
1 cup slivered red onion
1 tablespoon Dijon mustard
2 tablespoons soy sauce
3 tablespoons cider vinegar
2 teaspoons dark-roasted sesame oil

DIRECTIONS:
Trim and cut the green beans into 1-inch lengths. Cook in rapidly boiling water, about 5 minutes or until crunchy-tender.
Drain beans, immerse in cold water to stop the cooking until they are cool, then drain again. Mix mustard, soy sauce, vinegar and oil in a small bowl with a whisk until well blended. Toss the green beans with the ginger root, red onion and dressing.

NUTRITIONAL INFORMATION:
Servings: 4
Calories: 67
Total Fat: 2.5 g (61 %)
Total Carbohydrates: 11 g (29 %)
Dietary Fiber: 3 g
Protein: 2 g (9%)

NOTES:

131

Cucumber, Mango and Red Onion Salad

INGREDIENTS:
1 medium cucumber, peeled and thinly sliced
1 mango, pitted and cut into large dice
1 red onion, sliced into thin rounds
2 tablespoons lime juice
Salt to taste
3 tablespoons chopped cilantro
½ thinly sliced jalapeno pepper

DIRECTIONS:
Place the cucumber, mango and red onion in a medium bowl. Season to taste with the lime juice and salt. Garnish generously with cilantro leaves and the jalapeno pepper.

NUTRITIONAL INFORMATION:
Servings: 4 (1/2 cup)
Calories 52
Total Fat: 0 g (5 %)
Total Carbohydrates: 14 g (90 %)
Dietary Fiber: 2 g
Protein: 1 g (5 %)

NOTES:

INGREDIENTS:
3 Roma tomatoes, diced
1 ½ cups cucumbers, peeled and sliced
½ cup radishes, sliced thin
12 ounces romaine lettuce
½ avocado
2 tablespoons parsley, chopped
1 clove garlic, minced
1 tablespoon liquid hot pepper sauce
1 ½ tablespoons lemon juice
1 tablespoon olive oil

DIRECTIONS:
Prepare the vegetables. Tear Romaine lettuce into bite-sized pieces. In a blow, mix together avocado, cilantro, garlic, hot pepper sauce, lemon juice and olive oil until creamy. In larger serving bow, combine lettuce, tomatoes, cucumbers and radishes. Add desired amount of dressing and mix.

NUTRITIONAL INFORMATION:
Servings: 4
Calories: 98
Fat: 7 g (63 %)
Carbohydrates: 8 g (30 %)
        Dietary Fiber: 4 g
Protein: 4 g (7 %)

NOTES:

INGREDIENTS:
4 cups green beans, trimmed
2 cups chopped tomatoes
1 ½ teaspoons olive oil
½ teaspoon salt
¼ teaspoon freshly ground pepper
½ cup thinly sliced fresh basil
½ cup (2 ounces) crumbled feta cheese

DIRECTIONS:
Bring water to boil; cook beans until crisp-tender (5 minutes). Drain and rinse with cold water.
Combine tomato, oil, salt, and pepper in bowl.
Divide beans in 8 plates, top each with ¼ cup tomato mixture. Sprinkle each serving with one tablespoon sliced basil and 1 tablespoon cheese.

NUTRITIONAL INFORMATION:
Servings: 8
Calories: 54
Total Fat : 2.5 g (42 %)
Total Carbohydrates: 9 g (43 %)
Dietary Fiber: 2.5 g
Protein: 2.5 g (15 %)

NOTES:

INGREDIENTS:
1 pound green beans, trimmed
1 tablespoon sherry vinegar
1 ½ teaspoons olive oil
1 teaspoon Dijon mustard
¼ teaspoon salt
¼ teaspoon freshly ground black pepper
1 tablespoon sliced almonds, toasted

DIRECTIONS:
Cook beans in boiling water 4 minutes or until crisp-tender. Drain and plunge beans into ice water; drain well.
Combine vinegar, oil, mustard, salt and pepper in medium bowl, stirring with a whisk until well blended. Add beans to vinegar mixture and toss well to coat. Sprinkle with almonds.

NUTRITIONAL INFORMATION:
Servings: 4 (1 cup)
Calories: 63
Total Fat: 3 g (40 %)
Total Carbohydrates: 9 g (50 %)
Dietary Fiber: 4 g
Protein: 2.5 g (11 %)

NOTES:

Roasted Corn, Black Bean & Mango Salad

INGREDIENTS:
2 teaspoons canola oil
1 clove garlic, minced
1 ½ cups corn kernels
1 large ripe mango, peeled and diced
1 (15-ounce) can bleack beans, rinsed
½ cup chopped red onion
½ cup diced red bell pepper
3 tablespoons lime juice
1 small canned chipotle pepper, drained and chopped
1 ½ tablespoons chopped fresh cilantro
¼ teaspoon cumin
¼ teaspoon salt

DIRECTIONS:
Heat oil in a large nonstick skillet over medium-high heat. Add garlic and cook, stirring, until fragrant, about 30 seconds. Stir in corn and cook, stirring occasionally, until browned, about 8 minutes. Transfer the corn mixture to a large bowl. Stir in mango, beans, onion, bell pepper, lime juice, chipotle, cilantro, cumin and salt.

NUTRITIONAL INFORMATION:
Servings: 8 (1/2 cup)
Calories: 106
Total Fat: 2 g (14 %)
Total Carbohydrates: 21 g (73 %)
Dietary Fiber: 5 g
Protein: 4 g (13 %)

NOTES:

INGREDIENTS:
2 medium green bell peppers, cut into bite-sized chunks
2 medium red bell peppers, cut into bite-sized chunks
2 medium red onions, cut into bite-sized chunks
1 pint red cherry tomatoes
1 cup pitted kalamata olives, roughly chopped
Nonstick cooking spray
Salt and freshly ground black pepper
Juice of ½ lemon
½ cup feta cheese
¼ cup flat leaf parsley leaves, chopped

DIRECTIONS:
Preheat oven to 400 degrees F and spray large baking sheet with nonstick cooking spray.
Toss together peppers, onion, tomatoes and olives on the baking sheet, season to taste and roast in the oven until lightly brown and tender, about 15 minutes.
In large bowl, toss roasted vegetables together with lemon juice. Top with crumbled feta cheese and parsley.

NUTRITIONAL INFORMATION:
Servings:10 (1 cup each)
Calories: 96
Total Fat: 6 g (54 %)
Total Carbohydrates: 10 g (32 %)
Dietary Fiber: 2 g
Protein: 2 g (8 %)

NOTES:

Spinach, chickpeas and Cherry Tomatoes Salad

INGREDIENTS:
2 cups raw baby spinach
1 can (16-ounce) chick peas, rinsed and drained
1 cup cherry tomatoes, cut crosswise
1 tablespoon chopped parsley
2 tablespoons red wine vinegar
1 tablespoon olive oil
1 tablespoon freshly squeezed lemon juice
2 cloves garlic, minced
½ teaspoon lemon zest
¼ teaspoon freshly ground black pepper

DIRECTIONS:
Toss spinach, chickpeas, tomatoes and parsley in bowl.
Whisk all other ingredients together in small bowl. Pour over salad and toss to coat. Let stand at least 30 minutes at room temperature to blend flavors.

NUTRITIONAL INFORMATION:
Servings: 4
Calories: 142
Total Fat: 7 g (44 %)
Total Carbohydrates: 17 g (31 %)
Dietary Fiber: 6 g
Protein: 6 g (17 %)

NOTES:

INGREDIENTS:
3 large yellow peppers
3 medium tomatoes
⅓ cup crumbled Gorgonzola cheese
Watercress
2 tablespoons olive oil
2 tablespoons white wine vinegar
1 tablespoon chives
2 teaspoons basil, fresh
1 teaspoon raw sugar
½ tablespoon mustard, Dijon-style
⅛ teaspoon pepper, black

DIRECTIONS:
In a covered large skillet, cook sweet pepper rings in boiling water for 1 to 2 minutes or just until crisp-tender. Drain and cool. Cover and chill for 1 to 24 hours. Cut tomatoes in wedges.
In small bowl, whisk together oil. vinegar, chives, basil, sugar, mustard and pepper.
On a platter, arrange tomato wedge and pepper rings. Top with cheese and drizzle with dressing. Garnish with watercress.

NUTRITIONAL INFORMATION:
Servings: 8
Calories: 112
Total Fat: 9 g (71 %)
Total Carbohydrates: 8 g (26 %)
Dietary Fiber: 1 g
Protein: 1.5 g (4 %)

NOTES:

Zesty Chickpea Salad

INGREDIENTS:
¼ cup non-fat plain yogurt
1 teaspoon black pepper
½ red onion, minced
½ jalapeno pepper, thinly sliced
2 tablespoons cumin
19-oz. can chick peas, rinsed and drained
1 tablespoon lemon juice
¼ teaspoon salt
4 cups chopped romaine lettuce
4 cups spinach

DIRECTIONS:
In a large salad bowl, combine yogurt, black pepper, red onion, jalapeno and cumin.
Stir in chick peas and add the lemon juice. Mix well. Serve on the bed of greens.

NUTRITIONAL INFORMATION:
Servings: 4
Calories: 142
Total Fat: 7 g (44 %)
Total Carbohydrates: 17 g (31 %)
Dietary Fiber: 6 g
Protein: 6 g (17 %)

NOTES:

Dressings

Balsamic Vinaigrette

INGREDIENTS:
⅓ cup extra-virgin olive oil
⅓ cup balsamic vinegar
2 teaspoons chopped fresh thyme
¼ teaspoon salt
⅛ teaspoon white pepper
1 tablespoon chopped fresh basil

DIRECTIONS
Combine all ingredients in a screw-top jar and shake.

NUTRITIONAL INFORMATION:
Servings: 11 (1 tablespoon)
Calories: 58
Fat: 6.5 g (98 %)
Carbohydrates: 0.5 g (2 %)
Dietary Fiber: 0 g
Protein: 0 g (0 %)

NOTES:

Citrus Vinaigrette

INGREDIENTS
¼ cup orange juice
2 tablespoons sherry vinegar
2 tablespoons olive oil
1 tablespoon water
1 tablespoon honey
¼ teaspoon salt
¼ teaspoon pepper

DIRECTIONS:
Combine all ingredients in a screw-top jar and shake.

NUTRITIONAL INFORMATION:
Servings: 10 (1 tablespoon)
Calories: 33.5
Total Fat: 2.5 g (71 %)
Total Carbohydrates: 2.5 g (28 %)
Dietary Fiber: 0 g
Protein: 0 g (0 %)

NOTES:

INGREDIENTS:
6 ounces silken tofu (or soft tofu, drained)
2 tablespoons fresh lemon juice
1 tablespoon canola oil
½ teaspoon salt
¼ teaspoon pepper
1 tablespoon chopped fresh parsley
1 clove garlic, chopped
1 ½ tablespoons cider vinegar

DIRECTIONS:
Combine all ingredients in a blender container. Blend until well mixed.

NUTRITIONAL INFORMATION:
Servings: 8
Calories: 30
Total Fat: 2.5 g (70 %)
Total Carbohydrates: 1 g (15 %)
Dietary Fiber: 0 g
Protein: 1 g (15 %)

NOTES:

Red Pepper Vinaigrette

INGREDIENTS:
¼ cup apple juice
¼ cup cider vinegar
2 tablespoons chopped onion
2 cloves garlic, minced
½ teaspoon dried whole oregano
Pinches of rosemary and thyme
½ teaspoon dry mustard powder
½ teaspoon paprika
½ of a roasted red pepper

DIRECTIONS:
Combine all ingredients in a blender container. Blend until well mixed.

NUTRITIONAL INFORMATION:
Servings: 8
Calories: 8
Total Fat: 0 g (0 %)
Total Carbohydrates: 2 g (100 %)
Dietary Fiber: 0 g
Protein: 0 g (0 %)

NOTES:

Tomato Herb Vinaigrette

INGREDIENTS;
1 ½ cups peeled and finely chopped firm, ripe tomatoes
¼ cup minced green onions or chives
2 tablespoons minced fresh basil or tarragon (or 1 tablespoon dried herbs)
1 large clove garlic, finely minced
½ teaspoon raw sugar
½ teaspoon salt
¼ teaspoon freshly ground pepper
¼ cup balsamic vinegar
2 tablespoons olive oil
1 tablespoon Dijon mustard

DIRECTIONS;
Combine tomatoes, green onion, basil, garlic, sugar, salt and pepper in a medium bowl and stir well. Cover and let stand at room temperature 1 hour. Add vinegar, olive oil and mustard, and stir well.

NUTRITIONAL INFORMATION:
Servings: 24 (1 tablespoon)
Calories: 20
Total Fat: 1 g (45 %)
Total Carbohydrates: 2 g (40 %)
Dietary Fiber: 0 g
Protein: 0 g

NOTES:

Serious Salads (Main Dish)

Couscous Salad

INGREDIENTS:
1 can (14 ounces) fat-free chicken broth
¼ cup water
10 ounces couscous
1 tablespoon Dijon mustard
1 tablespoon lemon juice
¼ cup red wine vinegar
2 tablespoons olive oil
½ red or yellow pepper, diced
8 ounces cherry tomatoes, quartered
1 cucumber, diced
½ cup red onion, finely diced
4 ounces feta cheese, crumbled
Sea salt and freshly ground black pepper

DIRECTIONS:
Bring broth and water to a boil in medium saucepan. Remove from heat and stir in couscous. Cover and let sit for 5 minutes.
Whisk mustard, lemon juice and vinegar together; slowly add olive oil and whisk.
Transfer couscous to large bowl and fluff with fork to separate grains. Add tomatoes, cucumbers, green onions and feta cheese. Add dressing and toss. Add salt and pepper to taste.
Serve at room temperature.

NUTRITIONAL INFORMATION:
Servings: 12 (1/2 cup)
Per serving: 146 calories
Total Fat: 4.5 g (27 %)
Total Carbohydrates: 21 g (59 %)
Dietary Fiber: 2 g
Protein: 5 g (14 %)

NOTES:

Cranberry Couscous

INGREDIENTS:
1 cup whole wheat couscous
1 ½ cups fat free chicken broth
2 teaspoons cumin
Salt and freshly ground pepper to taste
1 tablespoon olive oil
1 medium onion, diced small
1 can chickpeas
½ cup dried cranberries, chopped

DIRECTIONS:
Heat chicken broth and cumin in medium-sized pan until it almost boils. Turn heat off and add couscous. Cover and let sit for 15 minutes. Meanwhile, heat 1 tablespoon olive oil in pan and add onion, sauté until translucent. Add cranberries and chickpeas and sauté one to two minutes.
Fluff couscous with a fork. Add cranberry mixture to couscous and stir.
Serve warm or cold.

NUTRITIONAL INFORMATION:
Servings: 12 (1/2 cup)
Calories: 135
Total Fat: 1.5 g (11 %)
Total Carbohydrates: 26 g (78 %)
Dietary Fiber: 3 g
Protein: 4 g (12 %)

NOTES:

INGREDIENTS:
1 pound skinless, boneless chicken breast halves
½ cup pecans
¼ cup red wine vinegar
2 tablespoons raw sugar
¼ cup olive oil
½ medium onion, minced
1 teaspoon ground mustard
1 teaspoon salt
¼ teaspoon ground white pepper
2 heads Bibb lettuce - rinsed, dried and torn
24 ounces salad greens
1 cup sliced fresh berries, any kind, or orange slices in the winter

DIRECTIONS:
Preheat the grill for high heat. Grill chicken 8 minutes on each side, or until juices run clear. Remove from heat, cool, and slice.
Place pecans in a dry skillet over medium-high heat and cook them pecans until fragrant, stirring frequently, about 8 minutes. Remove from heat, and set aside.
In a blender, combine the red wine vinegar, raw sugar, olive oil, onion, mustard, salt, and pepper. Process until smooth. Arrange lettuces on serving plates. Top with grilled chicken slices, berries, and pecans. Drizzle with the dressing to serve.

NUTRITION INFORMATION:
Servings: 6
Calories: 302
Total Fat: 20 g (58 %)
Total Carbohydrates: 15 g (18%)
Dietary Fiber: 5 g
Protein: 18 g (24 %)

NOTES:

INGREDIENTS:
1 teaspoon dried oregano
½ teaspoon garlic powder
¾ teaspoon black pepper, divided
½ teaspoon salt, divided
Nonstick cooking spray
1 pound skinless, boneless chicken breast, cut up in 1-inch cubes
5 teaspoons fresh lemon juice, divided
2 teaspoons tahini
1 teaspoon minced garlic
8 cups chopped romaine lettuce
1 cup peeled chopped cucumber
1 cup grape tomatoes, halved
6 pitted kalamata olives, halved
¼ cup feta cheese, crumbled

DIRECTIONS:
Combine oregano, garlic powder, ½ teaspoon pepper, ¼ teaspoon salt in a bowl. Heat a nonstick skillet over medium-high heat. Coat pan with nonstick cooking spray. Add chicken and spice mixture; cook, stirring, until chicken is done. Drizzle with 1 tablespoon juice; stir. Remove from pan.
Combine remaining juice, salt, pepper, yogurt, tahini and garlic. Stir well.
Combine lettuce, cucumber, tomatoes and olives. Place 2 ½ cups of lettuce mixture on each plate and top with ½ cup chicken and 1 tablespoon cheese. Drizzle each serving with 3 tablespoons yogurt mixture.

NUTRITIONAL INFORMATION:
Servings: 4
Calories: 209
Total Fat: 9 g (40 %)
Total Carbohydrates: 3.5 g (11 %)
Dietary Fiber: 3 g
Protein: 25 g (49 %)

NOTES:

INGREDIENTS:
2 limes
1 cup dry quinoa
1 ¼ cups water
2 tablespoons olive oil
1 ¼ teaspoons curry seasoning
¾ teaspoon salt
1 ½ cups shredded carrots
1 cup canned chickpeas, rinsed and drained
1 ½ cups thinly sliced green onions
¼ cup sliced almonds, toasted
¼ cup golden raisins
¼ teaspoon pepper

DIRECTIONS:
Zest one lime to produce 1 ½ teaspoons zest, then juice both limes. In a saucepan, combine 3 tablespoons lime juice, quinoa, water, 1 tablespoon olive oil, curry seasoning and ½ teaspoon salt. Bring to a boil. Reduce heat, cover and simmer for 15 to 20 minutes or until quinoa turns transparent and liquid is absorbed. Cool and place in a large bowl. Add carrots, chickpeas, green onions, almonds and currants. Toss. In a small bowl, combine remaining lime juice and olive oil, lime zest, ¼ teaspoon salt and the pepper. Whisk until well blended. Pour over quinoa mixture and toss.

NUTRITIONAL INFORMATION:
Servings: 6
Calories: 272
Total Fat : 9.5 g (31 %)
Total Carbohydrates: 41.5 g (59 %)
Dietary Fiber: 6.5 g
Protein: 8 g (10 %)

NOTES:

INGREDIENTS:
2 cups chopped mango
⅓ cup fresh orange juice
2 tablespoons olive oil
2 teaspoons grainy Dijon mustard
½ teaspoon salt
¼ teaspoon pepper
6 cups shredded Romaine lettuce
1 cup finely shredded cabbage
1 cup thinly sliced green onions
1 ½ cups cannellini beans, rinsed and drained
¼ cup pine nuts

DIRECTIONS:
In a blender, puree ¼ cup mango, orange juice, oil, mustard, salt and pepper.
In a large bowl, combine all other ingredients. Toss gently. Add vinaigrette and toss just before serving.

NUTRITIONAL INFORMATION:
Servings: 6
Calories: 216
Total Fat: 8 g (32 %)
Total Carbohydrates: 31.5 g (56 %)
Dietary Fiber: 7 g
 Protein: 8 g (12 %)

NOTES:

INGREDIENTS:

1 cup fresh green beans
6 cups torn mixed salad greens
1 (6-ounce) can chunk white tuna (packed in water), drained and broken into chunks
4 medium tomatoes, quartered
2 hard-cooked eggs, peeled and quartered
½ cup chopped fresh flat-leaf parsley
3 green onions, cut into ½" slices
4 anchovy fillets, drained, rinsed, and patted dry
¾ cup pitted ripe olives
Niçoise Dressing

DIRECTIONS:
Wash green beans; remove ends and strings. Leave beans whole or snap in half. In a covered medium saucepan, cook green beans in a small amount of boiling, lightly salted water about 5 minutes or just until tender. Drain and place in ice water until chilled; drain well. If desired, cover and chill for 2 to 24 hours. Place salad greens on a large platter or 4 serving plates. Arrange green beans, tuna, tomatoes, and eggs on the greens. Sprinkle with parsley and green onions. Top with olives. Drizzle Niçoise Dressing over all.

Niçoise Dressing: In a small bowl combine 2 tablespoons extra-virgin olive oil, 1 tablespoon white wine vinegar, ½ teaspoon Dijon-style mustard, ¼ teaspoon kosher salt, and ⅛ teaspoon freshly ground black pepper. Whisk together until combined.

NUTRITIONAL INFORMATION:
Servings: 4
Calories: 239
Fat: 14 g (53 %)
Carbohydrates: 11 g (17 %)
Dietary Fiber: 4 g
Protein: 18.5 g (31 %)

NOTES:

INGREDIENTS:
3 cups mixed greens
3 ounces shrimp, boiled and chilled
¼ cup sliced red pepper
¼ cup sliced green pepper
¼ cup sliced cucumber
2 tablespoons chopped green onions
2 tablespoons Tomato Vinaigrette (see Recipe)

DIRECTIONS:
Place all ingredients in large salad bowl. Toss and top with vinaigrette.

NUTRITIONAL INFORMATION:
Servings: 1
Calories: 119
Fat: 2 g (6 %)
Carbohydrates: 23 g (43 %)
Dietary Fiber: 5 g
Protein: 15 g (18 %)

NOTES:

Tuna, Asparagus and Feta Salad

INGREDIENTS:
4 cups romaine lettuce torn into pieces
2 plum tomatoes, cut into 8 pieces
1 cup steamed asparagus pieces
1 can (6 ounces) white albacore tuna, drained
2 oz. feta cheese, crumbled
1 tablespoon olive oil
1 tablespoon balsamic vinegar

DIRECTIONS:
Mix the romaine, tomato and asparagus. Add the tuna and feta cheese. Sprinkle with the olive oil and toss to coat. Add the balsamic vinegar and toss again.

NUTRITIONAL INFORMATION:
Servings: 2
Calories: 283
Total Fat: 14 g (44 %)
Total Carbohydrates: 11 g (14 %)
Dietary Fiber: 4 g
Protein: 30 g (42 %)

NOTES:

Tomato-Chickpeas Couscous Salad

INGREDIENTS:
¾ cup cooked couscous
1 large tomato, chopped
⅓ cup canned chickpeas, drained and rinsed
2 green onions, chopped
1 teaspoon olive oil
1 tablespoon lemon juice
1 tablespoon fresh chopped basil
4 cups mixed greens

DIRECTIONS:
Combine all ingredients but lettuce. Toss and serve on a bed of lettuce.

NUTRITIONAL INFORMATION:
Servings: 2
Calories: 177
Total Fat: 3.5 g (17 %)
Total Carbohydrates: 31.5 g (71 %)
Dietary Fiber: 6.5 g
Protein: 7 g (13 %)

NOTES:

Warm Chicken Salad with Pine Nuts

INGREDIENTS:
3 cups fat-free chicken broth
¾ cup balsamic vinegar
4 cloves garlic, peeled and halved
2 sprigs rosemary plus ½ teaspoon chopped bay leaf
2 boneless, skinless chicken breast halves (10 ounces), trimmed of fat
1 tablespoon extra-virgin olive oil
1 tablespoon chopped green onion
¼ teaspoon freshly ground black pepper
Salt to taste
6 cups torn mixed salad greens
1 medium-size red bell pepper, roasted and cut into thin strips
1 tablespoon pine nuts, toasted
1 tablespoon chopped fresh parsley

DIRECTIONS:
In a wide saucepan, combine broth, vinegar, garlic, fresh rosemary sprigs, and bay leaf.
Bring to a boil, reduce heat, and simmer 5 minutes. Add chicken breasts; cover and poach
gently for about 15 minutes or until no longer pink inside. Transfer to a cutting board and
keep warm. Boil the poaching liquid for 5 minutes, or until slightly reduced.
Strain; discard garlic, rosemary, and bay leaf, and pour ¼ cup poaching liquid into a small
bowl. Whisk in oil, green onion and pepper. Season with salt if desired.
In a large bowl, toss greens with 2 tablespoons of the oil mixture. Arrange on individual
plates. Carve chicken into thin slices and arrange over greens. Garnish with red pepper and
drizzle the remaining dressing over chicken and peppers. Sprinkle pine nuts, parsley, and
remaining fresh rosemary over the chicken.

NUTRITIONAL INFORMATION:
Serving: 2
Calories: 342
Total Fat: 16 g (43 %)
Total Carbohydrates: 18 g (17 %)
Dietary Fiber: 6 g
Protein: 33 g (40 %)

NOTES:

INGREDIENTS:
1 ½ cups quinoa
3 cups plus 3 tablespoons water
Salt
3 cups raw broccoli flowerets
12 cherry tomatoes, quartered
4 mushrooms, sliced
1 cup chopped carrot
3 tablespoons finely chopped peeled fresh ginger
2 tablespoons olive oil
2 tablespoons seasoned rice vinegar
2 teaspoons soy sauce
Salt and pepper to taste

DIRECTIONS:
In sieve, rinse quinoa with cold running water.
In 3-quart saucepan, combine quinoa, 3 cups water, and ½ teaspoon salt; heat to boiling over high heat. Reduce heat to low; cover and simmer 20 minutes or until water is absorbed. Transfer quinoa to large bowl. Meanwhile, cook broccoli until tender-crisp. Drain; add to quinoa in bowl. Add tomatoes and mushrooms.
In blender, combine carrot, ginger, olive oil, vinegar, soy sauce, remaining 3 tablespoons water, and ¼ teaspoon salt; blend until pureed. Add to quinoa, broccoli, and tomatoes and toss to combine. Serve salad warm or at room temperature.

NUTRITIONAL INFORMATION
Servings: 7 (1 cup each)
Calories: 196
Total Fat: 6 g (28 %)
Total Carbohydrates: 30 g (53%)
Dietary Fiber: 4 g
Protein: 4 g (8 %)

NOTES:

Side Dishes

"Kissing don't last;
Cookery do!"
George Meredith

Broiled Balsamic Mushrooms

INGREDIENTS:
2 tablespoons balsamic vinegar
2 tablespoons water
2 teaspoons olive oil
½ teaspoon dried thyme
12 ounces portabello mushrooms, trimmed and thickly sliced

DIRECTIONS:
Preheat broiler and line broiler pan rack with foil.
In large bowl, whisk together vinegar, water, oil and thyme. Add mushrooms and toss gently to coat. Arrange in a single layer on the rack and broil 3" from the heat for 2 minutes. Turn and broil for 2 minutes longer, or until golden.

NUTRITIONAL INFORMATION:
Servings: 4
Calories: 43
Total Fat: 2.5 (49 %)
Total Carbohydrates: 5 g (37 %)
Dietary Fiber: 1 g
Protein: 2 g (13 %)

NOTES:

INGREDIENTS:
1 ½ cups brown rice
2 ½ cups fat-free chicken broth
1 tablespoon olive oil
⅛ teaspoon salt
⅛ teaspoon ground black pepper
¼ cup minced fresh parsley
1 teaspoon grated lemon zest
½ teaspoon lemon juice
¼ cup minced fresh parsley
¼ cup chopped fresh basil
½ cup grated Parmesan
½ cup minced onion

DIRECTION:
Preheat oven to 375 degrees F and spread rice in 8-inch square glass baking dish.
Heat 1 tablespoon olive oil in medium nonstick skillet over medium heat until shimmering.
Add the minced onion and cook until translucent, about 3 minutes. Set aside.
Bring fat-free chicken broth to boil. Once boiling, immediately stir in salt and pour broth over rice. Stir onion mixture into rice. Cover baking dish tightly with doubled layer of foil. Bake rice 1 hour until tender.
Remove baking dish from oven and uncover. Stir in the pepper, parsley, basil, Parmesan, grated lemon zest and lemon juice. Cover with clean kitchen towel and let rice stand 5 minutes. Uncover and let rice stand 5 minutes longer.

NUTRITIONAL INFORMATION:
Servings: 6
Calories: 230
Total Fat: 5.5 g (21 %)
Total Carbohydrates: 38 g (67 %)
Dietary Fiber: 2 g
Protein: 7 g (17 %)

NOTES:

Caramelized Sweet Potatoes and Pumpkin Seeds

INGREDIENTS:
1 tablespoon pumpkin seeds
1 tablespoon olive oil
1 large sweet potato, peeled and cut into ½-inch dice
Salt and freshly ground pepper
1 tablespoon balsamic vinegar

DIRECTIONS:
In a dry skillet, toast pumpkin seeds over medium heat until fragrant and lightly browned, about 3 minutes. Set aside.
In large heavy skillet, heat 1/2 tablespoon oil over medium-high heat. Add sweet potato cubes and sauté, tossing, until lightly browned, about 5 minutes. Pour ¼ cup water into skillet, cover, reduce heat to low and cook until the sweet potatoes are tender, 5-7 minutes more. Mound in center of a platter.
Heat remaining oil in skillet. Add balsamic vinegar and cook until reduced by half, 30-60 seconds. Spoon over the sweet potatoes. Sprinkle toasted pumpkin seeds on top.

NUTRITIONAL INFORMATION:
Servings: 4
Calories: 106
Total Fat: 6 g (52 %)
Total Carbohydrates: 11 g (43 g)
Dietary Fiber: 1.5 g
Protein: 2 g

NOTES:

Chinese-Style Broccoli

INGREDIENTS:
1 tablespoon canola oil
4 cups broccoli flowerets
1 tablespoon soy sauce
2 garlic cloves, minced
1 teaspoon fresh lemon juice

DIRECTIONS:
Heat oil in a large wok or high-sided skillet over medium-high heat. Add broccoli and stir-fry for 2 minutes. Add soy sauce, garlic, and lemon juice; continue to stir-fry until broccoli is crisp-tender, about 5 minutes. Serve hot.

NUTRITIONAL INFORMATION:
Servings: 3
Calories: 74
Total Fat: 5 g (60 %)
Total Carbohydrates: 8 g (31 %)
Dietary Fiber: 3 g
Protein: 3 g (11 %)

NOTES:

INGREDIENTS:
14 cups cubed peeled apple
½ lemon
3 cups fresh cranberries
¼ cup raw sugar
¼ cup maple syrup
⅓ cup water
½ teaspoon ground cinnamon
Pinch fresh grated nutmeg

DIRECTIONS:
Place cubed apples in a large bowl; cover with cold water, squeeze juice from lemon half into bowl and place lemon half in bowl. Set aside.
Combine cranberries and remaining ingredients in a Dutch oven; bring to a boil, stirring occasionally. Cook 3 minutes or until cranberries pop.
Drain apple; discard lemon. Add apple to pan, cover, reduce heat and simmer 25 minutes or until apple is soft. Uncover, bring to a boil and cook 15 minutes. Mash apple mixture roughly with a potato masher. Pour into serving dish; cover and chill at least 2 hours.

NUTRITIONAL INFORMATION:
Servings: 20 (1/2 cup)
Calories: 67
Total Fat: 0.5 g (4 %)
Total Carbohydrates: 17 g (86 %)
Dietary Fiber: 5 g
Protein: 0 g (1 %)

NOTES:

INGREDIENT:
2 packages (10 ounces each) frozen spinach, thawed
2 green onions, minced
1 clove garlic, minced
⅓ cup fat-free sour cream
½ teaspoon salt
¼ teaspoon coarsely ground black pepper

DIRECTIONS:
In a skillet, heat the spinach over medium-high heat for about 5 minutes or until the liquid evaporates. Add green onions and garlic. Cook until tender. Reduce heat to low; add sour cream, salt and pepper, stirring until sour cream melts. Do not simmer.

NUTRITIONAL INFORMATION:
Servings: 6
Calories: 33
Total Fat: 0 g (4 %)
Total Carbohydrates: 6.5 g (74 %)
Dietary Fiber: 2 g
Protein: 3 g (23 %)

NOTES:

Garlic-Cauliflower "Mashed Potatoes"

INGREDIENTS:
1 head cauliflower, about 5 cups raw
2 teaspoons garlic powder
½ teaspoon sea salt
1 teaspoon basil
1 tablespoon olive oil

DIRECTIONS:
Steam or boil cauliflower. In food processor, pulse-chop cauliflower and seasonings until smooth as mashed potatoes. Add olive oil. Blend.

NUTRITIONAL INFORMATION:
Servings: 3 (1 cup)
Calories: 80
Total Fat: 5.5 g (60 %)
Total Carbohydrates: 7.5 g (17 %)
Dietary Fiber: 5 g
Protein: 3.5 g (15 %)

NOTES:

166

INGREDIENTS:
4 ripe red tomatoes
2 tablespoons olive oil
5 cloves garlic, minced
2 tablespoons fresh thyme
4 tablespoons Parmesan
House Seasoning: 1 cup salt, ¼ cup black pepper, ¼ cup garlic powder—mix and keep in air tight container

DIRECTIONS:
Cut tomatoes in halves, season with House Seasoning.
Heat oil in small frying pan over medium heat. Add garlic, cook until it starts to turn golden brown.
Set grill for high heat. Place tomatoes, cut side down on the grill and grill for 3-5 minutes; turn over, top with garlic mixture, cook three minutes.
Remove, top with thyme, house seasoning and Parmesan.

NUTRITIONAL INFORMATION:
Servings: 4
Calories: 114
Total Fat: 9 g (67 %)
Total Carbohydrates: 7 g (23 %)
Dietary Fiber: 5 g
Protein: 3 g (11 %)

NOTES:

INGREDIENTS:
1 (28 ounce) can whole tomatoes
1 medium onion, sliced
½ pound fresh green beans, sliced
½ pound fresh okra, cut into 1/2" pieces or 3/4 cup frozen okra
¾ cup finely chopped green pepper
2 tablespoons lemon juice
1 teaspoon chopped fresh basil, or 1 teaspoon dried basil, crushed
1 ½ teaspoons chopped fresh oregano leaves, or ½ teaspoon dried oregano, crushed
3 medium (7" long) zucchini, cut into 1" cubes
1 medium eggplant, pared and, cut into 1" cubes
2 tablespoons grated Parmesan cheese

DIRECTIONS:
Drain and coarsely chop tomatoes. Save liquid. Mix together tomatoes and reserved liquid, onion, green beans, okra, green pepper, lemon juice, and herbs. Cover and bake at 325 degrees F for 15 minutes. Mix in zucchini and eggplant and continue baking, covered, 60-70 more minutes or until vegetables are tender. Stir occasionally. Sprinkle top with Parmesan cheese just before serving.

NUTRITIONAL INFORMATION:
Servings: 18 (½ cup)
Calories: 40
Total Fat: 0.5 g (9%)
Total Carbohydrates: 8.5 g (77 %)
Dietary Fiber: 3 g
Protein: 2 g (15 %)

NOTES:

INGREDIENTS:
3 cups butternut squash, mashed halved lengthwise and seeded
¼ cup water
2 tablespoons pure maple syrup
3 tablespoons lemon juice
1 tablespoon grated lemon peel

DIRECTIONS:
Place squash cut side down in an ungreased 13 x 9" baking dish. Add water. Cover and bake at 350 degrees F for 50-60 minutes or until tender. Scoop out the squash and place in a food processor. Process until smooth. Add the syrup, butter, lemon juice and peel; beat until smooth.

NUTRITIONAL INFORMATION:
Servings: 6 (1/2 cup)
Per serving: 74 calories
Total Fat: 1 g (9 %)
Total Carbohydrates: 17 g (85 %)
Dietary Fiber: 3.5 g
Protein: 1.5 g (5 %)

NOTES:

INGREDIENTS:
2 tablespoons olive oil
3 cups chopped yellow onion (3 medium)
1 tablespoon raw sugar
6 cloves garlic, minced
2 teaspoons sea salt
2 teaspoons dried basil
1 ½ teaspoons dried oregano
1 teaspoon dried thyme
1 teaspoon freshly ground black pepper
2 tablespoons balsamic vinegar
2 cups fat-free chicken broth
3 (28-ounce) cans crushed tomatoes

DIRECTIONS:
Heat oil in large Dutch oven over medium heat. Add onion to pan and cook 4 minutes, stirring frequently. Add sugar and all spices. Cook 1 minute, stirring constantly. Stir in vinegar; cook 30 seconds. Add broth and tomatoes, bring to a simmer and cook over low heat for 55 minutes or until sauce thickens, stirring occasionally.

NUTRITIONAL INFORMATION:
Servings: 12 (1/2 cup)
Calories: 50
Total Fat: 1 g (18 %)
Total Carbohydrates: 8 g (64 %)
Dietary Fiber: 2 g
Protein: 1.5 g (12 %)

NOTES:

INGREDIENTS:
1 large onion, peeled and halved
3 cups dry pinto beans, rinsed
½ fresh jalapeno pepper, seeded and chopped
3 tablespoons minced garlic
5 teaspoons salt
1 ¾ teaspoons fresh ground black pepper
⅛ teaspoon ground cumin, optional
9 cups water

DIRECTIONS:
Place the onion, rinsed beans, jalapeno, garlic, salt, pepper, and cumin into a slow cooker. Pour in the water and stir to combine. Cook on High for 8 hours, adding more water as needed. Note: if more than 1 cup of water has evaporated during cooking, then the temperature is too high. Once the beans have cooked, strain them, and reserve the liquid. Mash the beans with a potato masher, adding the reserved water as needed to attain desired consistency.

NUTRITIONAL INFORMATION:
Servings: 15
Calories: 135
Total Fat: 0.5 g (3 %)
Total Carbohydrates: 25.5 g (53 %)
Dietary Fiber: 5 g
Protein: 8 g (17 %)

NOTES:

INGREDIENTS:
8 portabella mushroom caps
Nonstick cooking spray
½ teaspoon freshly ground pepper
¼ teaspoon salt
1 cup NEWAY™ marinara (see Recipe)
½ cup grated Parmesan Cheese

DIRECTIONS:
Preheat broiler. Remove brown gills from the undersides of portabella mushrooms using a spoon and discard them. Place mushroom caps, underside down, on a baking sheet coated with cooking spray. Broil for 5 minutes. Turn mushroom caps over; sprinkle evenly with salt and pepper. Top each cap with 2 tablespoons of NEWAY™ marinara and 1 tablespoon Parmesan cheese. Broil 3 minutes or until cheese melts.

NUTRITIONAL INFORMATION:
Servings: 8
Per Serving: 53 calories
Fat: 2 g (34 %)
Total Carbohydrates: 5 g (20 %)
Dietary Fiber: 1 g
Protein: 3.5 g (26 %)

NOTES:

INGREDIENTS:
40 asparagus spears, trimmed (about 2 pounds)
Nonstick cooking spray
¼ teaspoon kosher salt
⅛ teaspoon freshly ground black pepper
2 tablespoons butter
2 teaspoons soy sauce
1 teaspoon balsamic vinegar
Cracked black pepper and grated lemon rind (optional)

DIRECTIONS:
Preheat oven to 400 degrees. Arrange asparagus in a single layer on a baking sheet; coat with cooking spray. Sprinkle with salt and pepper. Bake at 400 for 12 minutes or until tender.
Melt butter in a small skillet over medium heat; cook 3 minutes or until lightly browned, shaking pan occasionally. Remove from heat; stir in soy sauce and balsamic vinegar. Drizzle over asparagus, tossing well to coat. Garnish with cracked pepper and rind if desired.

NUTRITIONAL INFORMATION:
Servings: 8 (5 spears each)
Calories: 51
Total Fat: 3 g (53 %)
Total Carbohydrates: 5 g (37 %)
Dietary Fiber: 2 g
Protein: 2 g (11 %)

NOTES:

Roasted Lemony Broccoli

INGREDIENTS:
2 cups broccoli
½ cup finely sliced green onions
1 teaspoon olive oil
Sea salt and freshly ground pepper to taste
Juice of ½ small lemon

DIRECTIONS:
Preheat oven to 450 degrees F.
Toss broccoli with green onions, oil, salt and pepper. Place on a large baking sheet and roast until broccoli is tender and brown on bottom, 10-12 minutes. Remove from oven and sprinkle with lemon juice. Toss gently and serve.

NUTRITIONAL INFORMATION:
Servings: 2
Calories: 59
Total Fat: 2.5 g (40 %)
Total Carbohydrates: 8.5 g (45 %)
Dietary Fiber: 4 g
Protein: 3.5 g (5 %)

NOTES:

INGREDIENTS:
1 pounds tiny new potatoes
2 tablespoons olive oil
Nonstick cooking spray
1 teaspoon rosemary
Salt and freshly ground black pepper to taste
4 plum tomatoes
½ cup pitted kalamata olives
3 cloves garlic, minced
¼ cup Parmesan cheese

DIRECTIONS:
Preheat oven to 450°F and spray a 9 x 12" baking pan with nonstick cooking spray.
Place potatoes in pan. In a small bowl, combine oil, rosemary, salt, and pepper; drizzle over potatoes, tossing to coat. Bake for 20 minutes, stirring once. Add tomatoes, olives, and garlic, tossing to combine. Bake for 5 to 10 minutes more or until potatoes are tender and brown on the edges and tomatoes are soft. Transfer to a serving dish. Sprinkle with Parmesan cheese.

NUTRITIONAL INFORMATION:
Servings: 6
Calories: 127
Total Fat: 7 g (42 %)
Total Carbohydrates: 18 g (50 %)
Dietary Fiber: 2 g
Protein: 3 g (8 %)

NOTES:

Rum-Whipped Sweet Potatoes

INGREDIENTS:
4 cups raw, cubed sweet potatoes
1 orange
½ ounce of rum, or a few drops rum flavoring
¼ teaspoon cinnamon
¼ cup brown sugar
Pinch of salt

DIRECTIONS:
Boil or microwave yams until soft. In food processor, place cooked yams, rum, cinnamon, sugar and salt. Halve the orange and squeeze juice and pulp into the processor as well. Whip until smooth.

NUTRITIONAL INFORMATION:
Serving: ½ cup
Calories: 115
Total Fat: 2 g (18 %)
Total Carbohydrates: 24 g (74 %)
Dietary Fiber: 2 g
Protein: 1 g (5 %)

NOTES:

Squash, Apple and Onion Tart
Andrea Hicks

INGREDIENTS:
1 tablespoon olive oil
1 large Spanish onion, sliced
2 cloves garlic, minced
2 teaspoons dried sage
¼ cup skim milk
2 large apples, sliced
2 cups butternut squash, seeded and sliced
Cinnamon, salt and pepper to taste
Nonstick cooking spray

DIRECTIONS:
Preheat oven to 375 degrees F and spray deep dish pie pan with nonstick cooking spray.
Half squash lengthwise, seed and slice (electric knife is useful!).
In heavy saucepan, heat oil. Stir in onions, garlic, salt and pepper. Cook covered on low heat for about 20 minutes. Add sage and milk, simmer 3-5 minutes or until thickened.
In prepared pan, spread onions in bottom. Overlap apple and squash slices. Pour milk over it all and liberally sprinkle with cinnamon.
Bake on upper rack for 15 minutes, then cover with foil and bake 30 minutes more.

NUTRITIONAL INFORMATION:
Servings: 8
Calories: 70
Total Fat: 2 g (25 %)
Total Carbohydrates: 13 g (70 %)
Dietary Fiber: 2 g
Protein: 1 g (5 %)

NOTES:

177

Squash Medley

INGREDIENTS:
2 small zucchini, thinly sliced, about 2 cups
1 medium tomato, chopped
1 cup ripe black olives, sliced
1 cup chopped onion
2 teaspoons olive oil
1 teaspoon lemon juice
¾ teaspoon garlic salt
¼ teaspoon dried oregano
⅛ teaspoon freshly ground pepper
2 tablespoons grated Parmesan cheese

DIRECTIONS:
Place vegetables on thick foil. Combine oil, juice and spices in small bowl and pour over veggies. Fold foil around vegetables and seal tightly.
Grill on medium heat for 30-35 minutes until vegetables are tender. Sprinkle with Parmesan cheese.

NUTRITIONAL INFORMATION:
Servings: 4
Calories: 105
Total Fat: 7.5 g (64 %)
Total Carbohydrates: 8 g (29%)
Dietary Fiber: 2.5 g
Protein: 3 g (10%)

NOTES:

INGREDIENTS:
1 tablespoon olive oil
2 tablespoons dried parsley
¾ teaspoon sea salt
½ teaspoon paprika
⅛ teaspoon crushed red pepper
4 red potatoes, each cut into 8 wedges (2 pounds)
Nonstick cooking spray
2 tablespoons grated Parmesan cheese

DIRECTIONS:
Preheat oven to 450 degrees F and coat a baking sheet with nonstick cooking spray.
Combine all ingredients except cheese in a large bowl; toss well. Arrange potatoes in a
single layer on the baking sheet.
Bake for 30 minutes or until golden. Sprinkle potatoes with Parmesan cheese, and bake an
additional 2 minutes or until cheese melts.

NUTRITIONAL INFORMATION:
Servings: 6 (1 cup)
Calories: 137
Total Fat: 3 g (19 %)
Total Carbohydrates: 24 g (71 %)
Dietary Fiber: 3.5 g
Protein: 3.5 g (8 %)

NOTES:

Stuffing with Cranberries

INGREDIENTS:
1 cup chicken broth
1 cup chopped celery
½ cup chopped onion
10 slices whole-wheat bread, toasted and cut into cubes (10 ounces)
¼ cup chopped parsley
1 teaspoon dried tarragon
½ teaspoon paprika
⅛ teaspoon ground nutmeg
½ cup chopped fresh cranberries
1 cup whole water chestnuts
1 cup chopped apple
Nonstick cooking spray

DIRECTIONS:
Preheat the oven to 350 F and lightly coat a 2-quart baking dish with nonstickcooking spray.
In a large skillet, heat the chicken broth over medium heat. Add the celery and onion and saute until the vegetables are tender, about 5 minutes. Remove from heat.
In a large bowl, combine the bread cubes, parsley, tarragon, paprika, nutmeg, cranberries, water chestnuts and chopped apples. Add the onion and celery mixture. Stir to mix evenly.
Spoon stuffing into the prepared baking dish. Cover with aluminum foil and bake for 20 minutes. Uncover and bake 10 more minutes. Serve immediately.

NUTRITIONAL INFORMATION:
Servings: 6 (½ cup)
Calories: 157
Total Fat: 2 g (12 %)
Total Carbohydrates: 30 g (75%)
Dietary Fiber: 5.5 g
Protein: 5.5 g (13 %)

NOTES:

INGREDIENTS:
1 large onion
4 cloves garlic, minced
2 tablespoons olive oil
3 cups shredded zucchini
1 (28 ounce) can chunked tomatoes
1 (14 ounce) can tomato puree
2-3 dashes hot sauce
1 teaspoon pepper
Fresh basil to taste
1 teaspoon salt
1 tablespoon Italian seasonings
1 teaspoon raw sugar

DIRECTIONS:
Gently cook onion and garlic in oil. Add remaining ingredients and simmer for 30 minutes.
Serve over whole-wheat pasta or as a pizza/lasagna sauce.

NUTRITIONAL INFORMATION:
Servings: 12
Calories: 64
Total Fat: 2.5 g (34 %)
Total Carbohydrates: 10 g (59 %)
Dietary Fiber: 2 g
Protein: 2 g (7 %)

NOTES:

Breakfast Anytime:
Eggs, Breads, Muffins
and All That Good Stuff

"We plan, we toil, we suffer—in the hope of what?
A camel-load of idol's eyes?
The title deeds of Radio City?
The empire of Asia?
A trip to the moon?
No, no, no, no.
Simply to wake just in time to smell coffee and bacon and eggs."
J.B.Priestly

Eggs

Asparagus and Mushroom Omelet

INGREDIENTS:
2 egg whites
2 tablespoons water
6 medium asparagus spears
¼ cup sliced white mushrooms
¼ cup shredded reduced-fat mozzarella cheese

DIRECTIONS:
Boil 1" of water in large skillet; add asparagus and cook, uncovered, just until tender-crisp.
Meanwhile in medium bowl, whisk together eggs and water until whites and yolks are completely blended.
Coat a 10" nonstick skillet with cooking spray. Heat skillet over medium-high heat until just hot enough to sizzle when drop of water is added. Pour in egg mixture. It should set immediately.
Lift the edges as the mixture begins to set to allow the uncooked portion to flow underneath. When top is set, fill one half of the omelet with asparagus, mushrooms and cheese. Fold the omelet in half over filling with spatula and slide onto a serving plate.

NUTRITIONAL INFORMATION:
Servings: 1
Calories: 139
Fat: 5 g (32 %)
Carbohydrates: 7 g (17 %)
Dietary Fiber: 2 g
Protein: 17 g (51 %)

NOTES:

INGREDIENTS:
1 egg
1 ounce grated low-fat cheese
1 tablespoon salsa
1 small whole wheat tortilla
Nonstick cooking spray

DIRECTIONS:
Preheat the oven to 350 degrees F.
Scramble the egg quickly in a small skillet with nonstick cooking spray. Fold in the salsa and cheese. Put the tortilla on a cookie sheet sprayed with nonstick cooking spray. Put the egg mixture on one half and fold over the other half to cover. Bake for 5 minutes or until tortilla is crisp.

NUTRITIONAL INFORMATION:
Servings: 1
Calories: 234
Total Fat: 13 g (49 %)
Total Carbohydrates: 15 g (20 %)
Dietary Fiber: 3 g
Protein: 17 g (30 %)

NOTES:

INGREDIENTS:
1 cup diced onion
¼ cup plus 1 tablespoon water, divided
1 teaspoon olive oil
4 egg whites and 1 egg
2 teaspoons chopped fresh herb combination (or 1/2 teaspoon dried herbs)
Coarse salt and freshly ground pepper
¼ cup fat free ricotta

DIRECTIONS:
Bring onion and ¼ cup water to a boil in a small nonstick skillet over medium-high heat. Cover and cook until the onion is slightly softened, about 2 minutes. Uncover and continue cooking until the water has evaporated, 1 to 2 minutes. Drizzle in oil and stir until coated. Continue cooking, stirring often, until the onion begins to brown, 1 to 2 minutes more. Pour in egg and egg whites, reduce heat to medium-low and continue cooking, stirring constantly with a heatproof rubber spatula, until the egg starts to set, about 20 seconds. Continue cooking, lifting the edges so uncooked egg flows underneath, until mostly set, about 30 seconds more. Reduce heat to low. Sprinkle herbs, salt and pepper over the frittata. Spoon cheese on top. Lift up an edge of the frittata and drizzle the remaining 1 tablespoon water under it. Cover and cook until the egg is completely set and the cheese is hot, about 2 minutes. Slide the frittata out of the pan using the spatula and serve.

NUTRITIONAL INFORMATION:
Servings: 2
Calories: 123
Total Fat: 2.5 g (19 %)
Total Carbohydrates: 10 g (31 %)
Dietary Fiber: 1.5 %
Protein: 24 g (47 %)

NOTES:

Breads

Banana Bread

INGREDIENTS:
3 very ripe bananas
¼ cup honey
¼ cup unsweetened applesauce
Nonstick cooking spray
1 teaspoon vanilla extract
1 ½ cups whole-wheat pastry flour
1 ½ teaspoons baking soda
¼ teaspoon salt
½ cup chopped walnuts

DIRECTIONS:
Heat the oven to 350 degrees F and spray loaf pan with nonstick cooking spray.
Mash the bananas and mix with the honey, ~~canola oil~~ applesauce and vanilla extract. Stir together the whole wheat pastry flour, baking soda and salt. Add the nuts. Blend the two mixtures and spoon into a prepared loaf pan.
Bake for 40 minutes, or until center is set.

NUTRITIONAL INFORMATION:
Servings: 12
Calories: 132
Total Fat: 3.5 g (27 %)
Total Carbohydrates: 24 g (64 %)
Dietary Fiber: 5 g
Protein: 3 g (9 %)

NOTES:

INGREDIENTS:
1 cup rolled oats
1 cup oat flour (Grind 1¼ cups oatmeal in a blender for 45 seconds)
¼ teaspoon salt
4 tablespoons cold butter
½ cup water
Nonstick cooking spray

DIRECTIONS:
Preheat oven to 400° and spray nonstick spray on a baking sheet.
Combine oats, oat flour and salt in a large mixing bowl. Cut butter into oat mixture with two knives
or pastry cutter. Stir in water, mixing with a fork. If necessary, add an extra teaspoonful or two.
Gather dough together with your hands in the bowl, kneading a few times. Roll out dough on a
lightly floured board to about ¼" thick, which makes a circle about 8" in diameter, cut into eight wedges. A
pizza cutter works well for this.
Place wedges on prepared baking sheet; bake 20-25 minutes, or until well set and slightly browned around the edges.

NUTRITIONAL INFORMATION:
Servings: 8
Calories: 138
Total Fat: 7 g (49 %)
Total Carbohydrates: 15 g (41 %)
Dietary Fiber: 2 g
Protein: 4 g (9 %)

NOTES:

INGREDIENTS:
1 cup oat flour
¾ cup yellow whole-grain cornmeal
2 teaspoons baking powder
½ teaspoon salt
1 cup fat-free buttermilk
2 tablespoons canola oil
1 large egg white, lightly beaten
Nonstick cooking spray

DIRECTIONS:
Preheat oven to 425 degrees F and spray an 8-inch square baking pan with nonstick cooking spray.
Combine flour, cornmeal, baking powder and salt. Make a well in center of mixture.
Combine buttermilk, oil and egg white; stir with a whisk. Add to flour mixture and stir just until moistened. Scrape mixture into the baking pan. Bake for 20 minutes or until a wooden pick inserted in center comes out clean. Cool in pan on a wire rack.

NUTRITIONAL INFORMATION:
Servings: 12
Calories: 87
Fat: 3.5 g (35 %)
Carbohydrates: 12 g (53 %)
Dietary Fiber: 1.5 g
Protein: 2.5 g (11 %)

NOTES:

INGREDIENTS:
1 cup rolled oats
2 cups whole wheat flour
2 teaspoons baking powder
½ teaspoon salt
1 ½ tablespoons honey
½ cup unsweetened applesauce
¾ cup skim milk
Nonstick cooking spray

DIRECTIONS:
Preheat oven to 450 degrees F and spray baking sheet with nonstick cooking spray.
Grind oatmeal in a food processor of blender. In large bowl, combine oatmeal, flour, baking powder and salt. In separate bow, dissolve honey in vegetable oil and then stir in the milk.
Combine both mixture and stir until soft dough is formed. Form the dough into a ball and place on baking sheet.
Bake in preheated oven for about 20 minutes, or until bottom of load sounds hollow when tapped.

NUTRITIONAL INFORMATION:
Servings: 12
Calories: 111
Total Fat: 1 g (6 %)
Total Carbohydrates: 23 g (79 %)
Dietary fiber: 3 g
Protein: 4.5 g (14 %)

NOTES:

Pumpkin Bread

INGREDIENTS:
1-29 oz. can of pumpkin
3 cups whole wheat flour
1 teaspoon vanilla
1 teaspoon baking soda
1 teaspoon baking powder
½ cup pure maple syrup
1 tablespoon pumpkin pie spice
1 cup raw sugar
2 eggs
Nonstick cooking spray

DIRECTIONS:
Preheat oven to 350 degrees F and spray 2 loaf pans with nonstick cooking spray.
Mix all ingredients and pour into prepared loaf pans. Bake for 1 hour, or until toothpick comes out clean.

NUTRITIONAL INFORMATION:
Servings: 24
Calories: 116
Total Fat: 1 g (9 %)
Total Carbohydrates: 25 g (77 %)
Dietary Fiber: 3 g
Protein: 3 g (10 %)

NOTES:

INGREDIENTS:
Nonstick cooking spray
3 cups whole-wheat flour
1 ½ cups raw sugar
1 teaspoon baking powder
1 teaspoon baking soda
3 teaspoons cinnamon
¼ teaspoon grated nutmeg
¼ teaspoon ground cloves
1 teaspoon salt
4 egg whites
1 cup unsweetened applesauce
2 cups grated zucchini, tightly packed
1 tablespoon vanilla extract

DIRECTIONS:
Preheat the oven to 325°F and spray two 8x 4" loaf pans with non-stick cooking spray.
Mix all ingredients, spoon pour into loaf pans and bake until the bread is golden brown and set in the center, about 50 to 60 minutes.

NUTRITIONAL INFORMATION:
Servings: 12
Per serving: 107 calories
Total Fat: 0 g (2 %)
Total Carbohydrates: 25 g (80 %)
Dietary Fiber: 2.2 g
Protein: 3 g (10 %)

NOTES:

Muffins

Apple Almond Muffins
Linda Stewart

INGREDIENTS:
1 cup wheat bran
¾ cup skim milk
1 cup whole wheat flour
1 teaspoon baking soda
1 teaspoon baking powder
1 teaspoon cinnamon
¼ teaspoon salt
1 egg white, beaten
½ cup fat free plain yogurt
⅓ cup honey
1 teaspoon almond extract
1 large Granny Smith apple, cored, peeled and grated
1/5 cup slivered almonds
Nonstick cooking spray

DIRECTIONS:
Preheat oven to 375 degrees F and spray the muffin pans with nonstick cooking spray.
Combine wheat bran and milk in a bowl and let soak 5 minutes. In large bowl, mix together
dry ingredients. In separate bowl. Whisk together egg, yogurt, honey, vanilla, grated apple
and wheat bran mixture. Mix yogurt mixture into flour mixture. Fold in slivered almonds.
Spoon batter into prepared muffin cups. Bake 18-20 minutes or until tops spring back when
lightly touched. Cool on wire rack.

NUTRITIONAL INFORMATION:
Servings: 16
Calories: 109
Total Fat: 1.5 g (13 %)
Total Carbohydrates: 22.5 g (75 %)
Dietary Fiber: 4 g
Protein: 4 g (12 %)

NOTES:

Joan Lockhart

INGREDIENTS:
1 cup wheat bran
¾ cup skim milk
⅔ cup whole wheat flour
1 teaspoon baking soda
1 teaspoon baking powder
¼ teaspoon salt
2 egg whites
½ cup unsweetened applesauce
¼ cup raw sugar
1 teaspoon vanilla
1 teaspoon cocoa
2 ounces dark 100 % cacao unsweetened chocolate, grated
Nonstick cooking spray

DIRECTIONS:
Preheat oven to 375 degrees F and spray non-stick muffin pans with cooking spray.
Combine wheat bran and milk in a bowl and let soak 5 minutes. In large bowl, mix together dry ingredients. In separate bowl, mix the other ingredients. Mix with milk and bran.
Spoon batter into prepared muffin cups. Bake 18-20 minutes or until tops spring back when lightly touched. Cool on wire rack.

NUTRITIONAL INFORMATION:
Servings: 12
Calories: 98
Total Fat: 2.5 g (23 %)
Total Carbohydrates: 20 g (66 %)
Dietary Fiber: 3.5 g
Protein: 3 g (12 %)

NOTES:

INGREDIENTS:
1 cup rolled oats
1 cup skim milk mixed with 2 tablespoons vinegar to make nonfat buttermilk
1 cup whole wheat flour
2 teaspoons baking powder
1 teaspoon baking soda
½ cup brown sugar
½ cup unsweetened applesauce
1 egg
1 apple, peeled and chopped
2 teaspoons cinnamon
Nonstick cooking spray

DIRECTIONS:
Preheat oven to 375 degrees F and spray 12 muffin cups generously with nonstick cooking spray.
Make the buttermilk. Pour oats over it. Let it rest.
In large bowl, combine together remaining dry ingredients. Stir in buttermilk mixture, applesauce, chopped apple, cinnamon and egg. Mix well. Pour batter in prepared muffin cups.
Bake in preheated oven for 30 minutes, until a toothpick inserted into center of muffin comes out clean.

NUTRITIONAL INFORMATION:
Servings: 12
Calories: 103
Total Fat: 0 g (0 %)
Total Carbohydrates: 21g (66 %)
Dietary Fiber: 4 g
Protein: 4 g (16 %)

NOTES:

Orange Almond Muffins
Janie McKirgan

INGREDIENTS:
1 cup wheat bran
¾ cup skim milk
⅔ cup whole wheat flour
1 teaspoon baking soda
1 teaspoon baking powder
2 tablespoons raw sugar
¼ teaspoon salt
1 egg, beaten
½ cup fat-free vanilla yogurt
⅓ cup honey
Zest of 1 orange
1 tablespoon fresh orange juice
1 teaspoon vanilla
1 teaspoon real almond extract
¼ cup ground almonds
Nonstick cooking spray
Topping: sprinkle each muffin with ½ teaspoon raw sugar before baking

DIRECTIONS:
Preheat oven to 375 degrees F and spray muffin pan with nonstick cooking spray.
Combine wheat bran and milk in bowl and let soak for 5 minutes. In a large bowl, mix dry ingredients together.
In separate bowl, mix egg, yogurt, honey, orange zest, orange juice, vanilla and almond extract. Add wheat bran mixture. Mix the flour mixture into the yogurt mixture. Fold in almonds.
Spoon batter into prepared muffin cups. Bake 18 to 20 minutes or until tops spring back when lightly touched. Cool on wire rack.

NUTRITIONAL INFORMATION:
Servings: 12
Calories:111
Total Fat: 2.5 g (28%)
Total Carbohydrates: 22 g (61 %)
Dietary Fiber: 3 g
Protein: 3.5 g (11 %)

NOTES:

INGREDIENTS:
½ peeled, seeded and cubed butternut squash (1 cup mashed)
1 cup old-fashioned oats
½ cup whole wheat flour
2 teaspoons baking powder
2 teaspoons baking soda
½ cup brown sugar
¼ teaspoon salt
2 teaspoons pumpkin pie spice
¾ cup skim milk
½ cup raisins
1 egg, beaten
Nonstick cooking spray

DIRECTIONS:
Preheat oven to 400 degrees F and spray a 12 cup muffin pan with nonstick cooking spray.
In a medium saucepan with enough water to cover, boil squash 20 minutes, or until tender.
Remove from heat, drain, and puree in a food processor.
In a large bowl, whisk together oatmeal, flour, baking powder, brown sugar, salt and
pumpkin pie spice. In a medium bowl, thoroughly mix together milk and egg. Stir in squash.
Fold the squash mixture into the flour mixture just until moistened and add raisins.
Spoon the batter into the prepared muffin pan, filling cups about ½ full.
Bake 20 minutes in the preheated oven, or until a toothpick inserted in the center of a muffin
comes out clean. Remove from muffin pan and cool on a wire rack.

NUTRITIONAL INFORMATION:
Servings: 12
Calories: 136
Total Fat: 1 g (9 %)
Total Carbohydrates: 28 g (76 %)
Dietary Fiber: 2 g
Protein: 4 g (12 %)

NOTES:

All That Good Stuff

Cranberry Muesli

INGREDIENTS:
½ cup fat-free yogurt
½ cup unsweetened cranberry juice
6 tablespoons old-fashioned rolled oats
2 tablespoons dried cranberry
1 tablespoon unsalted sunflower seeds
1 tablespoon wheat germs
2 teaspoons honey
¼ teaspoon vanilla extract
⅛ teaspoon salt

DIRECTIONS:
Combine yogurt, juice, oats, cranberries, sunflower seed, wheat germ, honey, vanilla and salt in medium bowl. Cover and refrigerate for at least 8 hours and up to 1 day.

NUTRITIONAL INFORMATION:
Servings: 2 (2/3 cup)
Calories: 197
Total Fat: 3.5 g (16 %)
Total Carbohydrates: 35 g (71 %)
Dietary Fiber: 3 g
Protein: 8 g (15 %)

NOTES:

INGREDIENTS:
2 ¾ whole wheat flour
2 tablespoons brown sugar
½ teaspoon sea salt
4 tablespoons baking powder
1 egg
3 cups skim milk
2 tablespoons melted butter

DIRECTIONS:
Mix and sift dry ingredients. Add beaten egg, milk and fat to make a thin batter. Add extra milk for thinner pancakes.
Drop on a preheated pan coated with cooking spray.

NUTRITIONAL INFORMATION:
Servings: 28 medium size pancakes
Calories: 58
Total Fat: 1 g (17 %)
Total Carbohydrates: 9.5 g (52 %)
Dietary Fiber: 1.5 g
Protein: 2 g (22 %)

NOTES:

Sweet Tooth for All

"Vegetables are a must on a diet.
I suggest carrot cake, zucchini bread, and pumpkin pie."
Jim Davis

Cookies

Chocolate Chip Biscotti

INGREDIENTS:
1 cup whole wheat Flour
½ cup raw sugar
¼ cup unsweetened cocoa
½ teaspoon baking soda
¼ teaspoon salt
3 egg whites
½ teaspoon vanilla
1 teaspoon honey
1 ounce NEWAY™ approved dark chocolate chips, chopped

DIRECTIONS:
Preheat oven to 350 degrees.
In a large bowl, mix together until blended the flour, sugar, cocoa powder, baking soda, and salt.
In a medium bowl, mix together the egg whites, honey, and vanilla. Add this to the flour mixture. Mix together until well combined. The dough will be sticky.
Lightly flour your hands and a surface. Roll the dough into 2-inch thick rope. Place the rope on a baking sheet. Press the dough rope to a 1" thick width. Bake for 25-28 minutes or until firm to the touch. Remove from oven and let it cool on baking sheet for 2-5 minutes. Place rope on a cutting board. Cut rope into ½" thick slices (about 16 slices). Place slices on the baking sheet with the cut sides facing up.
Bake for 8 minutes. Turn the biscotti on the other cut side for another 8 minutes or until dry.

NUTRITIONAL INFORMATION:
Servings: 16
Calories: 62
Fat: 1 g (17 %)
Carbohydrates: 13 g (70 %)
Dietary Fiber: 3 g
Protein: 2.5 g (14 %)

NOTES:

INGREDIENTS:
½ teaspoon cream of tartar
Dash of salt
6 large egg whites
½ cup raw sugar
¼ teaspoon vanilla extract
2 ounces flaked unsweetened coconut

DIRECTIONS:
Preheat oven to 250 degrees F.
Combine cream of tartar, salt and egg whites in a large bowl; beat with a mixer at medium speed until soft peaks form. Add sugar, 1 tablespoon at a time, beating at high speed until stiff peaks form. Add vanilla extract; beat just until blended—do not overbeat. Gently fold in coconut.
Drop by rounded tablespoons, 2 inches apart, onto 2 baking sheets covered with parchment paper.
Bake at 250 degrees F for 1 hour until very lightly browned and almost crisp, switching baking sheets and rotating front to back halfway through baking time. Remove from oven. Cool for 25 minutes (meringues will crisp as they cool).

NUTRITIONAL INFORMATION:
Servings: 32
Calories: 25
Total Fat: 1 g (38 %)
Total Carbohydrates: 3.5 g (53 %)
Dietary Fiber: 0 g
Protein: 0.5 g (9 %)

NOTES:

Granola Bar

INGREDIENTS:
1 egg
1 egg white
½ cup brown sugar
1 tablespoon canola oil
1 teaspoon cinnamon
¼ teaspoon salt
1 teaspoon vanilla extract
1 ½ cup old-fashioned rolled oats
⅔ cup dried cranberries, chopped
¼ cup pecans, chopped
1 tablespoon whole wheat or spelt flour
Nonstick cooking spray

DIRECTIONS:
Preheat oven to 350 degrees F. Spread oats on a baking sheet and bake, stirring
occasionally, for 15 to 18 minutes, until lightly browned and fragrant.
Reduce oven temperature to 325 degrees F and line an 8-by-11-inch pan with foil; coat with
nonstick cooking spray.
In a large bowl, whisk egg, egg white, brown sugar, oil, cinnamon, salt and vanilla extract.
Stir in toasted oats, dried cranberries, pecans and flour. Spread in prepared pan and bake
for 30 to 35 minutes, or until golden brown.
Cool. Cut into bars with a wet knife.

NUTRITIONAL INFORMATION:
Servings: 16
Calories: 94
Total Fat: 3 g (27 %)
Total Carbohydrates: 16 g (66 %)
Dietary Fiber: 1.5 g
Protein: 2 g (8 %)

NOTES:

INGREDIENTS:
1 ½ cups raw sugar
1 cup unsweetened applesauce
3 egg whites
¼ cup sour skim milk
1 ½ cups spelt flour
1 teaspoon baking soda
1 teaspoon baking powder
Juice and rind of 2 oranges (1 cup)
Nonstick cooking spray

DIRECTIONS:
Preheat oven to 350 degrees F and spray cookie sheet with nonstick cooking spray.
Mix raw sugar, unsweetened applesauce and egg whites well, then add sour milk and dry ingredients. Gently mix orange juice and rind in the batter. Drop the dough by spoonfuls on the prepared cookie sheet.
Bake in preheated oven for 10 to 12 minutes.

NUTRITIONAL INFORMATION:
Servings: 72 cookies
Calories: 27
Total Fat: 0 g (2 %)
Total Carbohydrates: 6.5 g (80 %)
Dietary Fiber: .5 g
Protein: 0.5 g (17 %)

NOTES:

Kashi® Crunch Cookie

INGREDIENTS:
4 cups Kashi® GOLEAN Crunch!™ cereal
1 teaspoon baking powder
2 egg whites
½ teaspoon cinnamon
½ cup dried currants or cranberries
Nonstick cooking spray

DIRECTIONS:
Preheat oven to 350°F.
Pulse cereal in a food processor about 10 times. Add baking powder, egg whites and cinnamon, and process for about 20 seconds or until the mixture is sticky and well blended. Stir in currants or cranberries.
Spray cookie sheet and a ¼-cup measuring cup with nonstick cooking spray.
Use the ¼ cup measuring cup to drop mounds of cookie mixture onto foil. Flatten the cookies by pressing down gently with a fork.
Bake for 10 minutes. Be careful not to over-bake; the cookies will still feel a little soft when you pull them out of the oven, but they will harden as they cool.

NUTRITIONAL INFORMATION: (with currants)
Servings: 15
Calories: 68
Total Fat: 1 g (13 %)
Total Carbohydrates: 13.5g (68 %)
Dietary Fiber: 3 g
Protein: 3 g (18 %)

NOTES:

INGREDIENTS:
1 cup spelt flour
1 cup walnuts, chopped
½ teaspoon baking soda
⅛ teaspoon fine sea salt
2 tablespoons unsalted butter at room temperature
¼ cup maple syrup
Cooking spray
1 teaspoon vanilla extract
¼ cup unsweetened applesauce

DIRECTIONS:
Preheat oven to 350 F and spray cookie sheet with nonstick cooking spray.
In food processor, combine flour, walnuts, baking soda and sea salt. Pulse until walnuts are finely chopped.
In large bowl, beat together butter and maple syrup with a wooden spoon until light and well blended. Beat in vanilla and add applesauce, beating well. Add dry ingredients and stir with the wooden spoon until blended.
Drop the dough by rounded teaspoons onto the cookie sheet.
Bake for 14 minutes or until cookies are just beginning to brown around the edges. Transfer to wire rack and let cool.

NUTRITIONAL INFORMATION:
Servings: 24
Per serving: 71 calories
Total Fat: 4 g (51 %)
Total Carbohydrates: 7 g (33 %)
Dietary Fiber: 1 g
Protein: 2 g (9 %)

NOTES:

INGREDIENTS:
Nonstick cooking spray
1 cup brown sugar
2 cups unsweetened applesauce
2 large egg whites
2 teaspoon vanilla
2 ½ cups canned chickpeas, drained and rinsed
4 ounces 60% cocoa bittersweet chocolate chips, or vegan chocolate chips
2 cups wheat bran
1 cup old-fashioned oats
1 teaspoon baking soda
¼ teaspoon salt

DIRECTIONS:
Preheat oven to 350 degrees F. Coat a baking sheet with cooking spray.
In large mixing bowl, beat sugar and applesauce. Beat in egg whites and vanilla, then chickpeas. Add wheat bran, oats, baking soda and salt and mix until a dough forms. Mix in chocolate chips.
Drop dough by tablespoonful onto baking sheet, spacing cookies about 2 inches apart.
Press gently with a fork to flatten. Bake until cookies are golden brown and set, about 20-25 minutes. Do not overbake. Transfer to rack to cool.

NUTRITIONAL INFORMATION:
Servings: 54
Calories: 50
Total Fat: 1 g (21 %)
Total Carbohydrates: 10 g (71 %)
Dietary Fiber: 2 g
Protein: 1.5 g (9 %)

NOTES:

Oatmeal Carrot Cookies

INGREDIENTS:
¾ cup unsweetened apple sauce
1 ¾ cups wheat flour
½ cup brown sugar
½ cup raw sugar
2 egg whites
1 teaspoon baking powder
½ cup raisins
½ teaspoon cinnamon
¼ teaspoon baking soda
¼ teaspoon ground cloves
1 teaspoon vanilla
2 cups old-fashioned oats
1 cup finely shredded carrots
Nonstick cooking spray

DIRECTIONS:
Preheat oven to 375 degrees F and spray cookie sheet with nonstick cooking spray.
Beat applesauce; add 1/2 of the flour, egg whites, all spices and vanilla and beat well. Stir in the rest of the ingredients. Dough will be stiff.
Drop dough by teaspoonfuls 2" apart on greased cookie sheet.
Bake at 375 degrees for 10 to 12 minutes.

NUTRITIONAL INFORMATION:
Servings: 66
Calories: 37
Total Fat: 0 g (5 %)
Total Carbohydrates: 8.5 g (86 %)
Dietary Fiber: 1 g
Protein: 1 g (9%)

NOTES:

Pecan Shortbread Cookies

INGREDIENTS:
6 ounces pecan halves
½ cup unsweetened apple sauce
¼ cup raw sugar
¼ cup brown sugar
1 teaspoon vanilla
1 teaspoon salt
1 ¾ cups spelt flour

DIRECTIONS:
Preheat oven to 350 degrees F with rack in the middle. Toast pecans in oven, then cool.
Pick out about 36 pecan halves for topping cookies and finely chop remainder.
Blend together applesauce, sugars, vanilla and salt in a bowl with a fork until combined well.
Stir in flour and chopped pecans until a soft dough forms (dough will be sticky). Form 1"
balls of dough and arrange 2 inches apart on 2 ungreased baking sheets. Flatten balls to ⅓"
thick using bottom of a glass moistened with water, then push a pecan half onto the center
of each cookie.
Bake 1 sheet at a time until edges are golden, about 20 minutes. Cool cookies on sheet 5
minutes, then transfer to a rack to cool.

NUTRITIONAL INFORMATION:
Servings: 36
Calories: 57
Fat: 3.5 g (52 %)
Carbohydrates: 6 g (38 %)
Dietary Fiber: 1 g
Protein: 1 g (8 %)

NOTES:

INGREDIENTS:
1 cup raw sugar
1 cup natural peanut butter
1 egg
Nonstick cooking spray

DIRECTIONS:
Preheat oven to 375°F and spray cookie sheets with nonstick cooking spray.
In a medium bowl, stir together the sugar, peanut butter and egg until well mixed. Using your hands, roll peanut butter mixture into 1" balls. Place 2 inches apart on prepared cookie sheets. Flatten each ball slightly with a drinking glass that has been moistened with water. Bake about 9 minutes or until edges are set and bottoms are lightly browned.

NUTRITIONAL INFORMATION:
Servings: 36
Calories: 64
Total Fat: 4 g (49 %)
Total Carbohydrates: 6.5 g (40 %)
Dietary Fiber: 0.5 g
Protein: 2 g (17 %)

NOTES:

INGREDIENTS:
1 cup old-fashioned rolled oats
1 cup spelt flour
1 teaspoon baking powder
½ teaspoon baking soda
¼ teaspoon salt
1 teaspoon cinnamon
½ teaspoon ginger
½ teaspoon allspice
½ cup brown sugar
2 egg whites
1 cup canned pure pumpkin
1 teaspoon vanilla
Nonstick cooking spray

DIRECTIONS:
Preheat oven 350 degrees and spray baking sheet with nonstick cooking spray.
In a medium bowl, using a whisk, combine flour, baking powder, baking soda, salt,
cinnamon, ginger and allspice.   In a large bowl, using an electric mixer, beat sugar, egg and
egg white, pumpkin and vanilla. Combine both mixtures, stirring gently until blended. Drop
spoonfuls of dough on the prepared cookie sheet. Bake for 12-14 minutes. Remove from
cookie sheet to a cooling rack.

NUTRITIONAL INFORMATION:
Servings: 32
Calories: 35
Total Fat: 0.5 g (9 %)
Total Carbohydrates: 7 g (76 %)
Dietary Fiber: 1 g
Protein: 1 g (13 %)

NOTES:

Custard-Textured Sweets

Baked Maple Custard

INGREDIENTS:
2 eggs
2 cups skim milk
2 tablespoons maple syrup
1 teaspoon vanilla
Ground nutmeg or cinnamon

DIRECTIONS:
Combine eggs, milk, maple syrup and vanilla. Whisk or beat until well blended. Pour into 4 glass custard cups. Sprinkle with nutmeg or cinnamon. Place the custard cups on a folded paper towel in a skillet with a tight fitting lid. Pour water into the pan, about 1 inch deep, and cover. Bring the water to a rolling boil. Remove pan from heat and let sit for 15 minutes. Serve warm or cold.

NUTRITIONAL INFORMATION:
Servings: 4
Calories: 105
Total Fat: 2.5 g (17 %)
Total Carbohydrates: 7 g (27 %)
Dietary Fiber: 0 g
Protein: 7.5 g (29%)

NOTES:

INGREDIENTS:
3 egg whites
1 egg
1 ½ cups skim milk
3 tablespoons raw sugar
1 teaspoon vanilla extract
⅔ cup cooked brown rice
⅓ cup chopped dates
Pinch of nutmeg or cinnamon

DIRECTIONS:
In a medium sized mixing bowl, combine egg whites, egg, milk, sugar and vanilla. Beat until combined but not foamy. Add cooked rice and chopped dates and mix well.
Pour rice mixture into a 1 ½ quart casserole dish. Place casserole dish in a baking pan then place in oven. Pour boiled water into baking pan around the casserole dish to a depth of about an inch.
Bake, uncovered at 325 F for 45 minutes or until a knife inserted halfway between the edge and the center comes out clean. Serve warm or chilled with a sprinkle of nutmeg or cinnamon.

NUTRITION INFORMATION:
Servings: 4
Calories: 174
Fat: 2 g (9 %)
Total Carbohydrates: 32 g (71 %)
Dietary Fiber: 2 g
Protein: 8 g (20 %)

NOTES:

INGREDIENTS:
12 ounces evaporated skim milk, undiluted
4 ounces skim milk
2 teaspoons vanilla
2 tablespoons raw sugar
Rosemary sprigs
2 egg whites
1 whole egg
5 teaspoons raw sugar and 5 sprigs of rosemary

DIRECTIONS:
Preheat oven to 350 degrees Fahrenheit. Whisk egg whites, egg, vanilla and 1 tablespoon raw sugar in a large bowl until well blended but not stiff, about 1 minute.
In heavy-bottomed saucepan, bring evaporated milk, skim milk, rosemary sprigs and 1tablespoon raw sugar to a boil over medium heat, stirring constantly. Cook until slightly thickened. Turn heat off.
Gradually add milk mixture to egg mixture, whisking constantly. Remove and discard rosemary sprigs.
Divide mixture among 5 4-oz ramekins. Arrange them in a roasting pan and add enough water to the pan to come halfway up the sides of the ramekins. Bake until set in the center, about 40 minutes. Cool ramekins on wire rack and cover them with plastic wrap. Refrigerate until very cold.
Heat broiler about 30 minutes before serving creme brulee. Sprinkle each ramekin with 1 teaspoon raw sugar. Return ramekins to roasting pan and add enough ice water to the pan to come halkway up the sides of ramekins. Broil 3 inches from heat for 2 to 3 minutes, or until sugar is melted and a thick, dark amber color. Stand one sprig of rosemary gently in each crème brulée.

NUTRITIONAL INFORMATION: CHANGE
Servings: 5
Calories: 92
Fat: 1 g (11 %)
Carbohydrates: 14 g (60 %)
Dietary Fiber: 0 g
Protein: 6 g (29 %)

NOTES:

INGREDIENTS:
1 cup chopped walnuts, divided
1 cup water
4 tablespoons cornstarch
6 cups cooked puréed winter squash (buttercup, banana, or hubbard)
½ cup brown sugar
2 ounces brandy
1 ½ teaspoons cinnamon
¾ teaspoon powdered ginger
½ teaspoon ground cloves
½ cup ground walnuts
Nonstick cooking spray

DIRECTIONS:
Preheat oven to 400 degrees F and spray a glass baking dish with nonstick cooking spray. In a blender, grind the walnut pieces until very fine. Add the water and blend on high speed for 2 minutes. Add the cornstarch or arrowroot powder and blend on low speed for 30 seconds. In a large mixing bowl, combine the squash purée, sugars, brandy, and spices. Add the walnut mixture to the squash and mix well. Pour squash puree the prepared baking dish. Top with the chopped walnuts. Bake for 50 minutes until lightly browned, cracked, and well-set.
Remove from the oven, cool, then refrigerate overnight to allow dessert to firm up. Serve cool or at room temperature.

NUTRITIONAL INFORMATION:
Servings: 12
Calories: 211
Total Fat: 13 g (52 %)
Total Carbohydrates: 21 g (38 %)
Diary Fiber: 4 g
Protein: 3.5 g (5 %)

NOTES:

Sweets with Fruit

Balsamic Strawberries

INGREDIENTS:
4 cups strawberries
½ tablespoon butter
3 tablespoons good balsamic vinegar

DIRECTIONS:
Clean and half strawberries.
Melt butter in large saucepan. Add balsamic vinegar. Stir. Add strawberries and cook until translucent red. Divide in four tall wine glasses.

NUTRITIONAL INFORMATION:
Servings: 4 (1 cup)
Calories: 60
Total Fat: 2 g (29 %)
Total Carbohydrates: 11 g (67 %)
Dietary Fiber: 3 g
Protein: 1 g (5 %)

NOTES: You can put these strawberries on NEWAY™ approved ice cream.

Banana Ice Cream

INGREDIENTS:
1 frozen banana
Half a cup of blueberries or any other unsweetened frozen fruit

DIRECTIONS:
Thaw banana just enough to be able to handle it. Slice it in thick slices. Put banana and berries in food processor. Process all ingredients briefly in a food processor until pureed and the consistency of ice cream. It should still be very cold. Scoop the puree into a container and freeze.

NUTRITION INFORMATION:
Servings: 2
Calories: 75
Total Fat: 0.5 g (5 %)
Total Carbohydrates: 19 g (91 %)
Dietary Fiber: 2.5 g
Protein: 0.5 g (4 %)

NOTES:

Berry Dessert Nachos

INGREDIENTS:
¾ cup light sour cream
1 teaspoon vanilla extract
¼ teaspoon cinnamon, ground
3 whole wheat tortillas
1 tablespoon butter
2 teaspoons raw sugar
3 cups raspberries
½ ounce slivered almonds
½ ounce grated dark chocolate

DIRECTIONS:
 Preheat oven to 400°F. In a small bowl, stir together sour cream, vanilla and 1/8 teaspoon cinnamon. Cover and chill while preparing tortillas. Lightly brush both sides of each tortilla with melted butter. In a small bowl, stir together sugar and 1/8 teaspoon cinnamon; sprinkle over tortillas. Cut each tortilla into 8 wedges; arrange on two ungreased baking sheets. Bake for 8 to 10 minutes or until crisp. Cool completely.
To serve, divide tortilla wedges among six dessert plates. Top with raspberries and/or blackberries and sour cream mixture. Sprinkle with almonds and grated chocolate.

NUTRITIONAL INFORMATION:
Servings: 6
Calories: 189
Total Fat: 10 g (46 %)
Total Carbohydrates: 23.5 g (42 %)
Dietary Fiber: 7 g
Protein: 5.5 g (11 %)

NOTES:

219

INGREDIENTS:
3 ripe pears, scrubbed, quartered, cored and thinly sliced
1 tablespoon brown sugar
½ ounce slivered almonds
½ cup low-fat vanilla yogurt

DIRECTIONS:
Place a broiler rack about 3 inches from source of heat. Heat the broiler. Arrange the pears in a shallow, flameproof dish in concentric circles, slightly overlapping each other. Sprinkle with the brown sugar. Broil until the brown sugar has caramelized and pears begin to brown, about 5 minutes.
Sprinkle with the almonds and broil for about 1 minute or until almonds turn golden. Serve warm, topping each serving with a dollop of vanilla yogurt.

NUTRITION INFORMATION:
Servings: 4
Calories: 122
Total Fat: 3 g (19 %)
Total Carbohydrates: 23.5 g (53 %)
Dietary Fiber: 3.5 g
Protein: 3 g (9 %)

NOTES:

INGREDIENTS:
½ cup dried apricots, chopped
1 medium apple, cored and grated
1 ¼ cups NEWAY™ approved granola
⅔ cup apple juice
1 tablespoon butter

DIRECTIONS:
Preheat oven to 375 degrees F. Place all ingredients in a large bowl and mix well. Press the mixture into a 8" round, nonstick shallow pie pan and bake for 35-40 minutes, or until lightly browned and firm. Score into wedges with a knife and leave to cool in the pan.

NUTRITIONAL INFORMATION:
Servings: 8
Calories: 127
Total Fat: 6 g (40 %)
Total Carbohydrates: 17.5 g (53 %)
Dietary Fiber: 2.5 g
Protein: 3 g (8 %)

NOTES:

Chocolate-Dipped Strawberries

INGREDIENTS:
2 ounces dark chocolate (70 % cocoa), chopped
1 ounce whipping cream
Dash of almond extract
8 large strawberries

DIRECTIONS:
Combine chocolate and whipping cream in a glass bowl. Microwave at medium power for 1 minute or until the chocolate melts, stirring after 30 seconds. Stir in the almond extract and cool slightly.
Dip each strawberry into the melted chocolate, allowing the excess to drip off. Place on a waxed paper-lined baking sheet. Refrigerate or freeze for about 15 minutes until the chocolate is set.

NUTRITIONAL INFORMATION:
Servings: 2
Calories: 172
Total Fat: 9.5 g (49 %)
Total Carbohydrates: 22 g (50 %)
Dietary Fiber: 4 g
Protein: 2 g (5 %)

NOTES:

INGREDIENTS:
Nonstick cooking spray
3 firm but ripe nectarines, halved, pitted
3 firm but ripe purple/black plums, halved, pitted
3 firm but ripe red plums, halved, pitted
6 metal skewers or thick wooden skewers soaked in water 30 minutes
2 tablespoons raw sugar

DIRECTIONS:
Spray the grill rack with nonstick cooking spray and prepare the barbecue (medium-high heat). Thread 1 piece of each fruit on each of 6 skewers so that the cut sides line up and lay flat. Sprinkle the sugar over the cut sides of the fruit. Let stand until the sugar dissolves, about 10 minutes.
Place the fruit skewers on the grill cut side down. Grill the fruit until it is heated through and caramelized, about 5 minutes. Transfer 1 fruit skewer to each plate and serve.

NUTRITIONAL INFORMATION:
Servings: 6
Calories: 85
Total Fat: 0.5 g (7 %)
Total Carbohydrates: 20.5 g (88 %)
Dietary Fiber: 2 g
Protein: 1 g (5 %)

NOTES:

Strawberry-Blueberry Crunch

INGREDIENTS:
¼ cup whole almonds plus 2 tablespoons sliced almonds
¼ teaspoon ground cinnamon
¼ teaspoon freshly ground nutmeg
1 tablespoon butter
2 cups sliced strawberries
1 cup blueberries
1 tablespoon raw sugar
½ cup part-skim ricotta cheese

DIRECTIONS:
Preheat the oven to 350°F.
In a blender or spice grinder, grind whole almonds until finely ground. In a small bowl, combine ground almonds, cinnamon, and nutmeg. Add margarine and stir to combine. Lightly coat an 8x8-inch baking dish with cooking spray. Place strawberries, blueberries, and raw sugar in the dish; toss to combine. Dot with ground nut mixture (it will not cover entire surface) and then sprinkle with sliced almonds.
Bake for 35 minutes, or until topping is golden and fruit is hot. Divide fruit among 6 dessert bowls and top each serving with 1 tablespoon of ricotta.

NUTRITIONAL INFORMATION:
Servings: 6
Calories: 115
Total Fat: 7 g (50 %)
Total Carbohydrates: 11 g (36 %)
Dietary Fiber: 2.5 g
Protein: 4 g (14 %)

NOTES:

Pies and Cakes

Crunchy Pumpkin Pie

INGREDIENTS FOR PIE CRUST:
1 cup rolled oats
¼ cup whole wheat flour
¼ cup ground almonds
2 tablespoons brown sugar
¼ teaspoon salt
3 tablespoons canola oil
1 tablespoon water
INGREDIENTS FOR PIE FILLING:
¼ cup brown sugar
½ teaspoon ground cinnamon
½ teaspoon ground nutmeg
¼ teaspoon salt
1 egg, beaten
4 teaspoons vanilla
1 cup canned pumpkin
⅔ cup evaporated skim milk

Preheat oven to 425º F. Mix oats, flour, almonds, brown sugar and salt together in small mixing bowl. Blend oil and water together in measuring cup with fork or small wire whisk until emulsified. Add oil mixture to dry ingredients and mix well. If needed, add small amount of water to hold mixture together.
Press into a 9-inch pie pan and bake for 8-10 minutes, or until light brown.
Turn the oven temperature down to 350º F. Mix sugar, cinnamon, nutmeg, and salt together in a bowl. Add egg and vanilla and mix to blend ingredients. Add pumpkin and milk and stir to combine. Pour into prepared pie shells.
Bake 45 minutes or until knife inserted near center comes out clean.

NUTRITIONAL INFORMATION:
Servings: 8
Calories: 190
Total Fat: 9.5 g (47 %)
Total Carbohydrates: 23 g (38 %)
Dietary Fiber: 3 g
Protein: 4 g (10 %)

NOTES:

INGREDIENTS:
1 cup spelt flour
5 tablespoons unsweetened cocoa powder
1 ½ teaspoons baking powder
1 teaspoon baking soda
¾ teaspoon cinnamon
¼ teaspoon salt
1 cup brown sugar
1 egg
2 egg whites
¼ cup unsweetened applesauce
1 teaspoon vanilla
½ teaspoon almond extract
1 cup low-fat sour cream
Nonstick cooking spray

DIRECTIONS:
Preheat oven to 350 degrees F.
In a small bowl, combine flour, cocoa, baking powder, baking soda, cinnamon and salt. Set aside.
In medium bowl, blend brown sugar, egg, egg whites and applesauce. Add vanilla, almond extract and sour cream. Beat on low until blended; gradually add flour mixture to sour cream mixture, beating on medium speed.
Spray an 8x8-inch pan with nonstick cooking spray. Spread batter into pan. Bake for 40 minutes or until toothpick comes out clean. Remove from oven. Cool in pan for 45 minutes.

NUTRITIONAL INFORMATION:
Servings: 12
Calories: 191
Total Fat: 5 g (23 %)
Total Carbohydrates: 35.5 g (68 %)
Dietary Fiber: 2 g
Protein: 3.5 g (7 %)

NOTES:

INGREDIENTS:
2 tablespoons unsalted butter
3 tablespoons unsweetened cocoa powder
½ cup blanched hazelnuts or almonds
½ cup raw sugar
3 ounces bittersweet chocolate
½ cup reduced-fat sour cream
2 egg yolks
1 tablespoon Frangelico or amaretto (optional)
1 teaspoon vanilla extract
½ teaspoon cinnamon
5 egg whites, at room temperature
¼ teaspoon salt
Fresh sliced strawberries (optional)

DIRECTIONS:
Preheat oven to 350 degrees F. Generously coat an 8" and 9" springform pan with 2 teaspoons of the butter and dust with 1 tablespoon of the cocoa. Don't tap out the excess cocoa; leave it in the pan.

In a food processor, process nuts with 1 tablespoon of sugar until finely ground. In top of a double broiler over barely simmering water, melt chocolate and remaining 4 teaspoons butter, stirring constantly until smooth. Remove from heat and place the chocolate mixture in a large bowl. Add nut mixture, sour cream, egg yolks, Frangelico or amaretto, vanilla, cinnamon, 5 tablespoons of sugar and remaining 2 tablespoons cocoa powder. Stir until well blended.

In another large bow with an electric mixer on high speed, beat the egg whites and salt until foamy. Gradually add remaining 2 tablespoons sugar, beating until stiff. Stir ¼ of the beaten whites into chocolate mixture to lighten it. Gently fold in the remaining whites. Spoon into the prepared pan and gently smooth top.

Bake for 30 minutes or until cake has risen, is dry on the top and a wooden pick inserted into the center comes out with a few moist crumbs. Cool on a rack until warm. The cake will fall dramatically. Loosen the edges of the cake with a knife and remove the pan sides. Serve with strawberries.

NUTRITIONAL INFORMATION:
Servings: 12
Per Serving: 162 calories
Fat: 10 g (54 %)
Total Carbohydrates: 16.5 g (37 %)
Dietary Fiber: 2 g
Protein: 4.5 g (10 %)

NOTES:

227

Karen's Brownies
Karen Pizarchik

INGREDIENTS:
9 tablespoons cocoa
1 cup unsweetened applesauce
1 cup spelt pastry flour
¾ teaspoon baking powder
¼ teaspoon sea salt
2 large egg whites
¾ cup honey
1 teaspoon vanilla
¼ cup ground walnuts
Nonstick cooking spray

DIRECTIONSL
Preheat oven to 350 degrees F and spray a 9x9 pan with nonstick cooking spray.
Mix cocoa and apple sauce together. Add in applesauce, flour, baking powder and salt. Mix at low speed. Add egg whites while mixing. Add honey and vanilla.
Pour batter in the prepared pan and top with ground walnuts. Bake about 30 minutes. Cut into 12 servings while warm.

NUTRITIONAL INFORMATION:
Servings: 12
Calories: 128
Total Fat: 2 g (12 %)
Total Carbohydrates: 29 g (78 %)
Dietary Fiber: 3 g
Protein: 3 g (8 %)

NOTES:

Submitted by Claire Pinkerton

INGREDIENTS:
2 tablespoons butter
1 cup unsweetened applesauce
½ cup brown sugar
¼ cup honey
3 medium ripe peaches cut into ¾ inch wedges
1 cup coarse yellow cornmeal
¾ cup whole wheat flour
1 teaspoon baking powder
1 ¼ teaspoons sea salt
1 large egg
2 egg whites
½ teaspoon vanilla
½ cup nonfat plain yogurt
2 tablespoons walnuts

DIRECTIONS:
Preheat oven to 350 degrees.
Melt the butter in a 9-inch cast iron skillet over medium heat, using a pastry brush to coat sides with butter as it melts. Sprinkle 1/8 cup brown sugar and the honey evenly over bottom of skillet and cook until sugar starts to bubble and turn golden brown, about 3 minutes. Arrange peaches in a circle at edge of skillet, on top of sugar/honey. Arrange the remaining wedges in the center to fill. Add walnuts to the top. Reduce heat to low, and cook until juices are bubbling and peaches begin to soften, 10 to 12 minutes. Remove from heat. Whisk cornmeal, whole wheat flour, baking powder and salt in medium bowl. In large bowl, beat applesauce and the rest of the brown sugar until fluffy. Add the egg and the egg whites, one at a time.   Mix in vanilla and yogurt, then beat in cornmeal mixture.
Drop large spoonfuls of batter over peaches, and spread evenly using an offset spatula. Bake until golden brown and a tester inserted in the center comes out clean (about 22 minutes).
Transfer skillet to a wire rack, and let it stand for 10 minutes. Run a knife or spatula around edge of cake. Quickly invert cake onto cutting board. Let cool before serving.

NUTRITIONAL INFORMATION:
Servings: 12
Calories: 165
Total Fat: 3.5 (19 %)
Total Carbohydrates: 31 g (72 %)
Dietary Fiber: 2.5 g
Protein: 4 g (9 %)

NOTES:

INGREDIENTS:
¼ cup finely chopped pecans
2 egg whites
⅛ teaspoon cream of tartar
½ teaspoon vanilla
5 tablespoons raw sugar

DIRECTIONS:
Preheat oven to 300 degrees F.
Combine egg whites with cream of tartar in mixing bowl. Beat until foamy. Gradually add raw sugar, beating until peaks form. Fold in chopped pecans and vanilla. Spoon into lighly greased 8" pie pan, building up ½" above edge of pan.
Bake for 45 minutes. Let it cool.

NUTRITIONAL INFORMATION:
Servings: 8
Calories: 59
Total Fat: 2.5 g (38 %)
Total Carbohydrates: 8 g (53 %)
Dietary Fiber: 0.5 g
Protein: 1 g (8 %)

NOTES:

INGREDIENTS:
Nonstick cooking spray
1 cup whole wheat flour
1 cup wheat bran
1 teaspoon baking soda
1 teaspoon ground ginger
1 teaspoon cinnamon
¼ teaspoon ground cloves
¼ teaspoon allspice
¼ teaspoon salt
2 egg whites
¾ cup brown sugar
1 cup unsweetened applesauce
½ cup nonfat plain yogurt
¼ cup molasses
2 teaspoons vanilla extract
1 tablespoon grated orange zest

DIRECTIONS:
Preheat oven to 375 degrees F and coat a 9x5-inch loaf pan with nonstick cooking spray.
In large bowl, mix flour, wheat bran, baking soda and spices. Set aside. In another bowl, beat sugar, applesauce, egg whites, yogurt, molasses, vanilla and orange zest. Add flour mixture and mix until smooth.
Pour batter into prepared pan. Bake until a toothpick comes out clean when inserted into the center of cake, about 45 minutes. Cool 5 minutes in the pan before turning the cake out onto rack to cool completely.

NUTRITIONAL INFORMATION:
Servings: 12
Calories: 131
Fat: 0.5 g (3 %)
Carbohydrates: 31.5 g (89 %)
Dietary Fiber: 3.5 g
Protein: 3 g (9 %)

NOTES:

Other Yummies

Cinnamon Tortillas

Submitted by Claudine Bothell

INGREDIENTS:
12 corn tortillas
Butter flavored nonstick cooking spray
Cinnamon
3 tablespoons raw sugar

DIRECTIONS:
Preheat oven to 375 degrees F.
Cut tortillas into 4 wedges. Place them on baking sheet and spray the top side of tortillas with cooking spray. Mix cinnamon to taste and sugar together, and sprinkle on tortillas. Bake in preheated oven for 8 to 10 minutes or until lightly browned and crisp. (Great with fruit salsa)

NUTRITIONAL INFORMATION:
Servings: 12
Calories: 61
Total Fat: 0.5 g (6 %)
Total Carbohydrates: 14 g (89 %)
Dietary Fiber: 1 g
Protein: 1 g (5 %)

NOTES:

Pumpkin Butter
Mindy Shank

INGREDIENTS:
1 small can (15 oz) pumpkin
½ cup unsweetened applesauce
½ cup raw sugar or to taste
¾ teaspoon pumpkin pie spice or to taste

DIRECTIONS:
Mix above ingredients together. Cover and cook on low for 1 hour.

NUTRITIONAL INFORMATION
Servings: 48 (1 tablespoon)
Calories: 13
Total Fat: 0 (11 %)
Total Carbohydrates: 3 g (87 %)
Dietary Fiber: 0 g
Protein: 0 g (2 %)

NOTES:

234

Drinks

"Water, taken in moderation, cannot hurt anybody."

Mark Twain

INGREDIENTS:
1 cup sliced carrots
1 cup orange juice
1 ½ cups ice cubes
½ teaspoon orange peel

DIRECTIONS:
In a covered small saucepan, cook carrots in a small amount of boiling water about 15 minutes or until very tender. Drain well. Cool.
Place drained carrots in a blender. Add finely shredded orange peel and orange juice. Cover and blend until smooth. Add ice cubes; cover and blend until smooth.
Pour into glasses. If desired, garnish with orange peel curls.

NUTRITIONAL INFORMATION:
Servings: 4
Calories: 42
Total Fat: 0 g (2 %)
Total Carbohydrates: 10 g (93%)
Dietary Fiber: 1 g
Protein: 1 g (6 %)

NOTES:

INGREDIENTS:
1 teaspoon instant coffee
½ cup skim milk
½ cup water
1 cup ice cubes
2 teaspoons raw sugar

DIRECTIONS:
Place all ingredients in blender. Blend until smooth and creamy.

NUTRITIONAL INFORMATION: ADD RAW SUGAR
Servings: 1
Calories: 76
Total Fat: 0 g (3 %)
Total Carbohydrates: 10 g (67 %)
Dietary Fiber: 0 g
Protein: 4 g (28 %)

NOTES:

Gazpacho Smoothie

INGREDIENTS:
1 small tomato, quartered
¾ cup tomato juice, chilled
2 tablespoons minced fresh cilantro leaves
1 small garlic clove, chopped
¼ jalapeno pepper, chopped
¼ teaspoon ground cumin
Juice of ½ fresh lime (about 1 tablespoon)
Small wedge of fresh lime and a cherry tomato for garnish (optional)

DIRECTIONS:
Freeze tomato in a plastic bag until hard, about 3 to 4 hours.
Place frozen tomato, juice, cilantro, garlic, jalapeno, cumin and lime juice in a blender. Purée until well blended and almost smooth. Pour into a tall tumbler filled with ice cubes. Garnish, if desired, with a small wedge of lime and a cherry tomato, speared on a short skewer and added to the glass like a swizzle stick.

NUTRITIONAL INFORMATION:
Servings: 1
Calories: 59
Total Fat: 0 g (7 %)
Total Carbohydrates: 14 g (85 %)
Dietary Fiber: 2 g
Protein: 2 g (10 %)

NOTES:

Honeydew-Kiwifruit Smoothie

INGREDIENTS:
2 cups cubed honeydew
1 small Granny Smith apple, peeled, cored, and cut up
1 kiwifruit, peeled and cut up
2 tablespoons raw sugar
1 tablespoon lemon juice
1 cup ice cubes
Honeydew and/or kiwifruit slices (optional)

DIRECTIONS:
In a blender container, combine honeydew, apple, kiwifruit, raw sugar, and lime juice. Cover and blend until smooth. Add ice cubes; cover and blend until cubes are crushed and mixture is slushy. Garnish with additional honeydew and/or kiwifruit slices, if desired.

NUTRITIONAL INFORMATION:
Servings: 4
Calories: 112
Total Fat: 1 g (5 %)
Total Carbohydrates: 22 g (88 %)
Dietary Fiber: 4.5 g
Protein: 3 g (7 %)

NOTES:

INGREDIENTS:
2 tablespoons cocoa powder
1 tablespoon raw sugar
2 tablespoons water
6 oz 1 percent milk
½ teaspoon vanilla
¼ teaspoon almond extract

DIRECTIONS:
In a small saucepan, stir together the cocoa powder and the sugar. Add the water and stir well. Cook over medium heat until the mixture comes to a low boil and the sugar dissolves. Stir in the milk, vanilla and almond extract. Reduce the heat to low and stir until warmed through.

NUTRITIONAL INFORMATION:
Servings: 1
Calories: 153
Total Fat: 3 g (20 %)
Total Carbohydrates: 27 g (59 %)
Dietary Fiber: 4 g
Protein: 9 g (21 %)

NOTES:

INGREDIENTS:
1 cup Cabernet Sauvignon or other dry red wine
1 cup water
1 16-ounce package frozen mixed berries
1 orange, thinly sliced
⅔ cup fresh orange juice (about 3 oranges)
¼ cup raw sugar
6 orange slices

DIRECTIONS:
Combine water, wine, berries and orange in large bowl. Cover and chill for 8 hours. Remove and discard orange.
Press berry mixture through sieve over bowl; discard solids.
Combine berry mixture, juice and sugar in dish, stirring until sugar dissolves. Cover and freeze 45 minutes. Stir with a fork, and repeat stirring every 45 minutes until completely frozen and slushy (about 4 hours).
Remove from freezer. Scrape mixture with fork until fluffy. Garnish with orange slices.

NUTRITIONAL INFORMATION:
Servings: 6 (3/4 cup ice and 1 orange slice)
Calories: 105
Total Fat: 0 g (2 %)
Total Carbohydrates: 20 g (71 %)
Dietary Fiber: 2 g
Protein: 1 g (3 %)

NOTES:

Index

A

B

C

E

F

G

H

I

K

L

M

O

P

Q

R

S

T

V

W

Z

2040197

Made in the USA